TRUE CRIME KILLERS

VOLUME 4

Ben Oakley

SELECT TITLES BY BEN OAKLEY

FICTION

HARRISON LAKE INVESTIGATIONS
The Camden Killer
The Limehouse Hotel
Monster of the Algarve

HONEYSUCKLE GOODWILLIES
The Mystery of Grimlow Forest
The Mystery of Crowstones Island

SUBNET SF TRILOGY
Unknown Origin
Alien Network
Final Contact

NONFICTION

TRUE CRIME
Bizarre True Crime Series
Monsters of True Crime Series
True Crime Killers Series
Orrible British True Crime Series
The Monstrous Book of Serial Killers
Year of the Serial Killer

OTHER NONFICTION
The Immortal Hour: The True Story of Netta Fornario
Suicide Prevention Handbook

As a thank you for adding this book to your collection, we would like to offer you a FREE eBook for simply signing up to our mailing list. Along with a free book, you'll get weekly updates from the world of true crime brought to you by truecrimelists.com, and early book release notifications so you can be the first to get them at an introductory price, exclusively for subscribers.

Visit WWW.TRUECRIMELISTS.COM and click on FREE BOOK from the menu.

Copyright © 2023 Ben Oakley.

First published in 2023 by Twelvetrees Camden.

This edition 2023.

The right of Ben Oakley to be identified as the
Author of the Work has been asserted by him in accordance
with the Copyright, Designs and Patents Act 1988.

Visit the author's website at www.writetheplanet.co.uk

All rights reserved. No part of this book may be reproduced, or stored in a retrieval system, or transmitted in any form or by any means, electronic, mechanical, photocopying, recording, or otherwise, without express written permission of the publisher.

Each case has been fully researched and fact-checked to bring you the best stories possible and all information is correct at the time of publication. This book is meant for entertainment and informational purposes only.

While the publisher and author have used their best efforts in preparing this book, they make no representations or warranties with respect to the accuracy or completeness of the contents of this book. Neither the publisher nor the author shall be liable for any loss of profit or any other commercial damages, including but not limited to special, incidental, consequential, personal, or other damages.

The author or publisher cannot be held responsible for any errors or misinterpretation of the facts detailed within. The book is not intended to hurt or defame individuals or companies involved.

ISBN: 978-1-915929-19-8

Cover design by Ben Oakley. Images by Marina Luisa.

For information about special discounts available
for bulk purchases, sales promotions, book signings,
trade shows, and distribution, contact
hello@twelvetreescamden.co.uk

Twelvetrees Camden Ltd
71-75 Shelton Street, Covent Garden
London, WC2H 9JQ

www.twelvetreescamden.co.uk

True Crime Killers Volume 4

The Blackout Killer 15

Queen of Blood.. 29

Murder at the Tom Tackle Pub... 41

Murder at the Metropolitan Opera 53

Dennis Nilsen: Serial Killer 61

The Evil Kingdom of Ervil LeBaron 75

Devil-Worshipping Camden Ripper 83

Charlie Chop-off 93

The Murder of Colette Aram 103

Killer Author 111

Jack the Stripper 121

The Horrors of Snowtown 133

The Collector 145

Playboy Bunny and the Schoolgirl 159

Ossett Exorcist Murder... 169

The Unsolved Murder of Ann Heron 177

Stoned Butcher of Tompkins Park 187

Lesbian Vampire Killer 197

18 real-life stories of serial killers and murderers with solved and unsolved killings from the USA, UK, Europe, and beyond.

Thank you very much for choosing this book for your collection! The true crime community is one I've fallen in love with over the years and I'm truly grateful for your support. To readers new and old, I raise my glass to you. In fact, it's down to my readers that this new series exists at all.

The mission behind TRUE CRIME KILLERS is as simple as it sounds, to share with you stories of real-life murders and the killers behind them. The cases are laid out in a concise, easy to read format, with all the facts and information you need. If you want a 300-page read on each case, this is not that book.

This is a true crime anthology series with 18 stories in each volume. Inside each volume you'll discover serial killers and murderers with solved and unsolved killings from the USA, UK, Europe, and beyond. Some you know, some you don't.

Many of the other series' released through Twelvetrees Camden are general true crime anthology books. They include the whole gamut, from murders to robberies and frauds to cybercrime. But TRUE CRIME KILLERS has one focus – murder.

Which needless to say means some of the stories contain descriptions of such an act. Where other books go all in on the gore, there is some restraint shown here – as much as is possible. But this is not a book about fluffy rabbits, it's a book about humans killing other humans, so expect a little darkness to come your way.

Let's take a journey through the history of murder from the UK to the USA and discover an evil kingdom run by a cult leader, an unsolved bikini murder, the true urban legend of Charlie Chop-off, Jack the Stripper, an author who wrote a novel about his crimes, a devil-worshipping ripper, Britain's worst serial killer, a stoned butcher, murder at the Met, and other real-life horror stories.

First, a warning.

Due to the nature of this book and the subject it discusses, there are depictions of murder included in some of the stories. **This is from the outset of this book.** If you know what you are getting yourself into and know what real-life killers likely do, then let us proceed.

Here are previews of the 18 real-life true crime stories within these blackened pages.

The Blackout Killer

During wartime London, as the German bombs were raining down, a serial killer was at work who brought a new kind of darkness to the cold and lonely streets of the British Capital.

Queen of Blood

Queen of the Vampires, castles, baths of blood, hundreds of victims, brutal slayings, legend, myth, and the worst female murderer in human history, welcome to the world of Elizabeth Bathory.

Murder at the Tom Tackle Pub

A young woman was brutally attacked and murdered outside a popular Southampton pub, resulting in a 30-year-long miscarriage of justice and the creation of Operation Iceberg.

Murder at the Metropolitan Opera

A violinist playing for the Metropolitan Opera vanished during the intermission only to be found murdered the following morning by a killer the media had dubbed The Phantom of the Opera.

Dennis Nilsen: Serial Killer

The sickening tale of British serial killer Dennis Nilsen, who killed 15 young men, and dissected some of their remains – before flushing them down the toilet and blocking the sewers with flesh.

The Evil Kingdom of Ervil LeBaron

A polygamous cult leader ordered the murders of at least 25 people, many from beyond the grave, in a tale of fear, control, and a mission to create the Kingdom of God on Earth.

Devil-Worshipping Camden Ripper

A devil-worshipping serial killer brutally murdered and dismembered at least three sex workers before dumping their body parts in canals and bins around Camden.

Charlie Chop-off

A serial killer in New York gained the name of Charlie Chop-off, for attacking young boys and mutilating their genitals, in an urban legend born from real life.

The Murder of Colette Aram

A confident killer murdered a 16-year-old girl and escaped justice for 25 years until advancements in DNA technology captured him, in the first case to be profiled on Crimewatch.

Killer Author

A detective reads a self-published fiction novel and discovers similarities to a real murder three years earlier, along with clues in the book that only the real killer would have known.

Jack the Stripper

If Jack the Ripper has gripped imaginations for over 100 years, then the story of Jack the Stripper in 1960s London, is enough to send chills to the darkest parts of your soul.

The Horrors of Snowtown

In Snowtown, a master manipulator convinced others to help him commit serial murder and dispose of their victims' bodies in barrels of acid, leaving 12 dead, and a town forever tainted by infamy.

The Collector

There is perhaps no serial killer more inhuman than The Kansas City Butcher, who inflicted such terrible tortures on his victims that the term 'monster' has never been so appropriate.

Playboy Bunny and the Schoolgirl

A Playboy Bunny and a schoolgirl were attacked and killed in two separate incidents in London six months apart, by the same killer who has never been identified.

Ossett Exorcist Murder

A loving husband, thought to be possessed by 40 demons, became the subject of an all-night exorcism, and less than two hours later; ripped his wife and dog to pieces with his bare hands.

The Unsolved Murder of Ann Heron

On the hottest day of the century, a woman sunbathing in her bikini had her throat cut by an unidentified attacker, then left in a pool of blood for her husband to find.

Stoned Butcher of Tompkins Park

A self-confessed marijuana guru dismembered his roommate, boiled the remains, and made soup from her brains – which he ate and shared with unsuspecting homeless people.

Lesbian Vampire Killer

A lesbian lover of all things occult claimed to survive off the blood of animals before convincing her friends she was a vampire who needed to kill to satisfy her craving for the red stuff.

The Blackout Killer

During wartime London, as the German bombs were raining down, a serial killer was at work who brought a new kind of darkness to the cold and lonely streets of the British Capital.

There is nothing worse than a city in fear of bombs falling from the sky, except perhaps a serial killer who took advantage of London's darkest hour to feed an evil desire for cold-blooded murder.

Known as the Blackout Killer or the Wartime Ripper, 27-year-old Gordon Cummins finally snapped and went on a killing spree across London that left six women dead and two severely injured, who barely managed to escape his clutches.

Coming just fifty years after the infamous Jack the Ripper murders, Cummins was seen as a new ripper, carving his way through the streets of

London. Most of the murders took place in February 1942 but he was also suspected of killing two more a few months earlier in October 1941.

The air raids across Britain's major cities led to enforced blackout measures at night, blanketing the cities in darkness. It was under this cover of night that the Blackout Killer roamed the wartime streets seeking his innocent victims.

The blackouts had been imposed on various cities including London from September 1939 and were put in place to prevent enemy aircraft from being able to identify targets by sight. The blackouts remained in place until some restrictions were lifted in September 1944 as the German war machine weakened.

What set Cummins apart from the rest of his dark peers, was the brutality with which he carried out many of his murders. Some of the victims were so badly mutilated that police first thought they had been victims of a German bomb.

Born at the tail-end of the First World War, North Yorkshire-raised Cummins spent his childhood under the watchful eye of hard-working parents. His father ran a school for mentally challenged teenagers, and his mother was a housewife to four children.

Cummins had an unremarkable childhood but sought a career in chemistry before moving to Newcastle when he was 18 to take a job as an industrial chemist. Due to his poor time-keeping and anti-social behaviour, most-likely developed from his family's closeness to the delinquent school, he failed to keep down a job for more than a few months.

When he was 20, Cummins moved to London and took various jobs but found himself drawn into the large social life the city offered. His love for clubs, bars, and London women, led to him developing a persona for himself that lifted him from his working class roots to something he believed was more desirable.

He worked on a posh London accent and told wild stories of nights with multiple women and a fake heritage designed to show others how better he was than them. His extravagant persona was funded by petty theft, lifting him from his beer-swigging peers into a champagne lifestyle.

At 21, Cummins joined the Royal Air Force and his posh persona led to many nicknames including The Duke and The Count. Though he annoyed most of his comrades with tales of grandeur, he trained hard enough to be selected for flight duty by the RAF selection board.

He also married Marjorie Stevens in 1936 but they never had children and their marriage was more out of convenience than love. She would continue to believe her husband was innocent of any crimes right up until her own death many years later.

Shortly before his arrest, Cummins was due to report for duty at an Air Crew Receiving Centre in Regent's Park, where he would have ultimately sat behind the controls of a Spitfire. But the Duke had gone down a path of murder and brutality that to this day raises the hairs on the back of the neck.

During the time of the first London murders in October 1941, Cummins was stationed in Colerne, Wiltshire, but whenever he went on leave, would head straight for central London to use prostitutes and revel in his own tales of magnificence and showmanship.

On the morning of 14th October 1941, following a bombing raid, workmen were searching through the rubble of a bombed house in Hampstead Road, close to Regents Park, when they stumbled upon a body. It was not unusual to find bodies in London during the war but there was something different about this one.

On top of some debris was the nude body of 19-year-old secretary Maple Churchward but she didn't show any signs of having been hurt during the bombing. Unsure of what they were looking at, the workmen called in the police, who confirmed that Maple had been strangled to death with her own knickers.

Despite being found nude, she had not been sexually assaulted. Police learned that Maple commonly slept with British servicemen, sometimes for money, other times for fun. She had last been seen at a bar in nearby Camden the previous evening.

Four days later, on the 17th, 48-year-old Edith Humphries was found by a friend lying in bed suffering from severe wounds. She had been stabbed in the head, hit with a heavy object multiple times, and her throat had been cut.

Edith was alive when she was rushed to hospital but died shortly after. There was no forced entry to her home and due to the closeness of both women's murders, police suspected the same killer had been responsible. Edith too was seen at a Central London bar the night before her murder.

Due to the severity of the war over London, the two murders were put on the backburner. During the following three months, Cummins was stationed at RAF St. John's Wood, commonly known as RAF Regents Park – a perfect location for him to escalate the murders.

On 8th February 1942, after a brief visit to his wife in nearby Southwark, Cummins headed out into war-torn London. A day later, another victim was found dead in an air-raid shelter. 41-year-old pharmacist Evelyn Hamilton was last seen drinking wine celebrating her 41st birthday at Marble Arch.

As she walked back to her boarding house, Cummins befriended and lured her to the air-raid shelter, where he became violent. He ripped off her clothes and manually strangled her to death. The autopsy showed that she tried to fight him off but was not sexually assaulted.

Her body was found by an electrician the following morning. Police discovered her handbag had been stolen, which may have contained upwards of £80, worth over £4,000 today. They learned that she was leaving London for Lincolnshire the next day and was winding up her personal affairs.

That same evening on 9th February, 34-year-old married nightclub hostess and prostitute Evelyn Oatley was approached by Cummins as she waited outside a restaurant in Shaftesbury. Just before midnight, the pair were seen entering an apartment building at 153 Wardour Street by another tenant.

The same tenant heard Oatley's radio turned up loud after midnight as Cummins was killing her and mutilating her body. He beat and strangled her into unconsciousness before cutting her throat from ear to ear. He then stripped her and laid her flat on the bed with her head hanging over the edge.

Then, with a razor blade, tin opener, and piece of a broken mirror, Cummins cut up her body, before raping her with an electric torch and curling tongs. Evidence found at the scene suggested he had used a total of seven blades to slice her body, which was found the next morning by electric meter workers.

Already tainted by the horrors of war, police found fingerprints on the tin opener, mirror, and other items belonging to Oatley. But when they checked the fingerprints on the police database, there was no match, and for good reason – Cummins had never been arrested or convicted of a crime.

Which makes his sudden killing of many women that much stranger. On the next day, the 11th, 43-year-old prostitute Margaret Florence Lowe was murdered at her flat in Gosfield Street, Marylebone. She had last been seen by a neighbour in the early hours of the morning, accompanied by a client.

The same neighbour heard the client leave about an hour later, whistling away to himself, as if he'd had a night of fun. Lowe's body wouldn't be found until two days later when her 15-year-old daughter arrived home to find her on a bloody bed.

Her nude body had been positioned in such a way that she was on her back with her legs apart and knees bent upward. She had been brutally beaten to death and strangled with a silk stocking. And if police thought Oatley's murder was horrific, it was nothing compared to Lowe's.

Cummins had mutilated Lowe, partly when she was alive, but mostly after she had died. He used a razor blade, kitchen knife, dinner knife, and a fire poker, to stab and slice her body. All four weapons were left embedded in her body or nearby on the bed.

Her stomach had been sliced open with such severity that her organs were exposed, along with multiple lacerations and cuts to her groin. A large wax candle had also been inserted into her. That the suspect walked away from the scene whistling happily sent chills down the investigators spines.

Fingerprints were lifted and matched those from the Oatley crime scene. Autopsies confirmed the suspect was left-handed, which Cummins was, but he was able to hide himself away in the arms of RAF Regent's Park.

One day after Lowe's horrific death, on 12th February, 25-year-old prostitute Catherine

Mulcahy was attacked by Cummins in her own home, after he had paid for her services. As Mulcahy stripped, Cummins attacked her and pushed her to the bed attempting to strangle her.

But Mulcahy was strong enough to fight him off and ran screaming from the flat. She later claimed that Cummins's eyes had changed from a well-to-do gentleman to a monster within seconds. Cummins exited the flat and tried to give her more money then fled before police arrived.

It was perhaps a fortunate case of luck that Cummins had forgotten to put back on his RAF belt, which was found in Mulcahy's apartment. The same evening, Cummins hooked up with 32-year-old prostitute Doris Jouannet, who took him back to her flat in Bayswater. She had referred to Cummins as a client she called '*The Captain*'.

The following day, Jouannet's husband with the help of a friend who was a police officer, broke down her bedroom door and discovered her nude body on the bed she used to entertain clients. The same brutality had been inflicted on Jouannet,

She had been strangled with a silk stocking, her jaw had been broken off due to the savagery of the attack, and her body had been mutilated with various sharp instruments, including a razor blade and multiple knives. Some of the flesh underneath her breasts had been carved off.

Once again, fingerprints taken from the scene matched those of the other murders. But police were already closing in due to Cummins having left the RAF belt at Mulcahy's flat.

The press initially gave little service to the story of the murderer, but with the killings so close together, Cummins was referred to as the Blackout Killer, and the following day made headlines across the entire country.

Even with police investigating him, and the press writing about the murders, for some reason known only to Cummins, he just couldn't stop killing, and less than a day after Jouannet's murder, he attacked another woman.

On the 13th, Cummins lured Margaret Heywood to join him for a drink in a bar in Piccadilly. When they left the bar, he attempted to forcibly direct Heywood to a nearby air raid shelter but she tried to fight him off. Cummins then pushed her into a doorway and strangled her into unconsciousness.

The attack was stopped when a passing beer bottle deliveryman spotted Cummins rifling through Heywood's handbag. The deliveryman came to the rescue forcing Cummins to flee, and in doing so he left behind his RAF gas mask and rucksack in the doorway. To cover himself later, Cummins stole another serviceman's gas mask and rucksack.

Fortunately, Heywood survived the attack and would later be able to identify Cummins. When police got hold of the gas mask and rucksack, they contacted the local RAF bases who ultimately led them to Cummins, due to the issue numbers on the military gear.

On Valentine's morning, Cummins was arrested but concocted a fake story that he was out drinking whisky with another serviceman whose name he coincidentally couldn't recall. He claimed to have no memory of attacking Heywood but wished to apologise to her if he had done.

While he was under arrest for committing grievous bodily harm, detectives realised they could have the Blackout Killer in custody, so they jumped into full-on investigatory mode to prove it.

The RAF Regent's Park passbook was signed by Cummins on all the nights that the murders and attacks happened, but fellow servicemen claimed they all had each other's backs and falsified documents with pencil should any one of them return after a military-enforced curfew.

Police later discovered that Cummins and other servicemen would sneak out of the base at night and not return until the early hours. When police searched his belongings they found most of the proof they were looking for.

Cummings had been taking souvenirs from each of his victims including a metal cigarette case belonging to Oatley along with a picture of her mother. There were traces of blood on one of his unwashed shirts, and his military uniform had traces of brick dust only found in the air raid shelter were Hamilton's body was found.

But more importantly, all the fingerprints belonging to the suspect in the four February murders were a match with Cummins. They also discovered that new £1 notes had been given to Mulcahy by her attacker. Investigators tracked the serial numbers and discovered the notes were brand new and had been issued via the RAF base to Cummins.

Heywood identified Cummins in a line-up and the police had everything they needed to lay multiple counts of murder at his feet. In front of them was not only one of the most brutal killers of 1940s London but a terrifying serial killer who offered no real motive for his crimes beyond circumstance.

Cummins still maintained his innocence when he was charged with murder on the 16th of February and put together various stories to lay the blame at the feet of other servicemen who had '*clearly*' swapped RAF-issued clothing and accessories with him to pin the blame on him.

In April 1942, Cummins went on trial for the murder of Oatley and pleaded not guilty. With all the witnesses, autopsies, and forensic evidence, there was no way Cummins was going to get away with it.

He was found guilty of the murder of Oatley, and in the interests of the British public, was sentenced to death. On 25th June 1942, Cummins was led to the gallows at Wandsworth prison where he was hanged. He maintained his innocence right up until the end.

He was eventually linked with the other murders, the two in October 1941 and three in February 1942. That he was already sentenced to death meant that any other convictions would not have changed the ultimate outcome.

Cummins was the only convicted murderer to be executed during an air raid. He remains one of Britain's most curious and brutal serial killer's, having claimed one more victim than Jack the Ripper, bringing darkness to a city where there were already horrors at every turn.

Queen of Blood

Queen of the Vampires, castles, baths of blood, hundreds of victims, brutal slayings, legend, myth, and the worst female murderer in human history, welcome to the world of Elizabeth Bathory.

The name of Bathory invokes images of a woman bathing in the blood of virgins, which would be horrific enough even in the realm of horror movies, where the legend has perpetuated. Unsettling then that the truth is even worse than the mind can endure.

When tales of her evil escaped her domain, she was ultimately not even sent to trial, instead being locked up in a windowless room in her castle, to rot until her eventual death in 1614, when she was 54-years old.

Her legend in the realm of Vampirism is second only to that of Count Dracula himself. Born in

1560 to the wealthy Bathory family, in Transylvania, Hungary. They ruled Transylvania as if it were an independent principality, such was the power they wielded.

Though Transylvania is now part of Romania, from the year 1003 to 1918, the region was part of historical Hungary, until the Austria-Hungary alliance was destroyed in the First World War, leading to the Union of Romania.

Witness accounts of the time suggested the Blood Countess may have killed up to 650 people, with the very lowest figure given as 80, of which she was charged. So what happened to the once innocent Elizabeth that led to her killing up to 650 people?

In her formative years, up until the age of 10, Elizabeth was known to have suffered from multiple seizures which modern-day research suggests would have been the consequence of epilepsy.

It is claimed in some circles, that her parents were actually related and had given birth to Elizabeth through their inbreeding. Inbreeding has been common among humans for at least 2,000 years, predominantly in Northern Africa, rural Europe, and the Middle East.

In the 16th Century, when Elizabeth was a child, the cure for conditions similar to the seizures of epilepsy were – how to put this – bizarre. The blood of a seemingly healthy person was applied to the lips of the sufferer. After the seizure ended, the sufferer would be fed a mix of healthy blood and grounded-up human skull.

All of this when Elizabeth was a mere child. It's not too big of a stretch to suggest using the blood of others would have been a way to make her feel better, a possible reason why she killed. It also would have had a psychological impact far greater that many at the time would have realised.

She was also witness to the severe beatings of servants and was once known to laugh out loud at the punishment of a servant whose crime had been stealing. It was said that the man's punishment was to be sewn into the body of a horse.

And yet, it wasn't the worst thing that Elizabeth would experience in her childhood.

When Elizabeth was 10-years-old, she was engaged to a member of another wealthy and aristocratic Hungarian family, a 15-year-old Count named Ferenc Nádasdy. In that time period, many proposed marriages of this sort were mostly political arrangements between rich families.

At the age of 13, Elizabeth became pregnant by a lover who was not part of the aristocratic circles, a peasant boy from the local villages. She gave birth to a baby boy and apparently gave the child away in secrecy. When Nádasdy found out, he tracked down the family and ordered the baby be castrated and torn apart by dogs.

On 8th May 1575, when she was 15, Elizabeth married Nádasdy at a ceremony said to have been host to over 4,000 guests. As Elizabeth's family was of a higher social standing, she refused to change her last name, and her new husband took the name of Bathory.

Elizabeth had been sexually active since the age of 10 and was known to have taken secret lovers in her family's castle when Nádasdy was away. Because Nádasdy was a soldier, and an ambitious one at that, he was often away on war campaigns and other military actions.

The young couple split their time between Castle Sárvár and the Castle of Csejte, with Csejte now being located in modern-day Slovakia. Elizabeth was trained on how to run the estates in her husband's absence.

Elizabeth's wedding gift was the Castle of Csejte, set against the Carpathian mountains. This included the large country house and 17 local villages – something that may have proved vital to her getting away with so many murders.

In 1578, when Elizabeth was 18, her husband, then 23, led the Hungarian troops to war and would continue to fight against the Ottoman empire up until his death in 1604. This meant that Elizabeth was left mostly alone to run his business affairs and the estates of both their families.

After her husband left for war, Elizabeth took many lovers, mostly from the villages, to satisfy her intense sexual desires. She ended up having at least four children with her husband, though some claim they were illegitimate offspring. Regardless, they were looked after by the same Governess who had looked after Elizabeth, who had little to do with her own children's lives.

Nádasdy died in 1604 after damage to his legs suffered in war. But unknown to Nádasdy, Elizabeth had already been killing, it wasn't until his death that the murders and stories of torture escalated rapidly.

By 1602, whispers around the villages were already being spread of something untoward happening at the Castle of Csejte. Servants were going missing and Elizabeth was hiring new servants on a regular basis with no details of what had happened to the previous ones.

Initially, many people were not too concerned, as unfortunately in the 16th and 17th Centuries, peasants were seen as disposable, and their lives expendable. Any questions brought to Elizabeth were dispelled easily enough on account of her wealth and familial position.

A position that would allow her to torture, maim, and kill without consequence.

Shortly after Nádasdy's death, and due to the rumours that had been circulating, a Lutheran minister named István Magyari suggested Elizabeth had been committing atrocities, but it took another six years for them to be taken seriously.

In 1610, King Matthias II assigned György Thurzó, the Palatine of Hungary (an official feudal investigator), to investigate the stories that were coming out of Bathory's domain. What Thurzó heard while building a case would horrify him and others until the end of their days.

At first, Elizabeth was accused of killing her servants but later of killing young girls who had been sent to her castle by unsuspecting family members, to learn good manners. It was suggested to Thurzó that Elizabeth believed drinking the blood of young girls would preserve her youthfulness and looks.

Witnesses inside the castle said that Elizabeth would use scissors to stab and bite their breasts, faces, hands, and legs. She would stick hot needles into their lips, under their fingernails, and burn them with hot metal items such as coins and keys. Others she would beat with clubs and let them starve to death.

Other tortures included pouring ice water over the naked bodies and leaving them in the courtyard to freeze to death. She would cover some in honey to be eaten by ants and insects, along with sewing their lips together, and biting off chunks of flesh from their faces.

One of her more popular tortures was to use her beloved scissors to slice open the skin between her victim's fingers. But as the witness accounts went on, the stories became more unreal and absurd.

Some witnesses accused her of cannibalism and blood drinking and others claimed they had seen her have sex with the devil himself. She was accused of Satanism, witchcraft, and practising black magic. Ultimately, she bathed in the blood of her victims.

By 1611, Thurzó had recorded over 300 witness statements of varying degrees from servants, villagers, and people known to Elizabeth. He laid charges at her feet, accusing her of killing – or being associated with the death of – 80 girls. When he arrived at the castle, he recorded seeing the dead body of a young girl, and a living girl being used as *'prey'* within the castle walls.

One witness, who claimed to have close ties with Elizabeth and assisted her with *'collecting'* the girls, said that Elizabeth had a diary which detailed the names of her victims. It was said the book, which is now conveniently lost to time, listed the names of 650 victims.

One of Elizabeth's more trusted servants who worked in the care of her children, was later convicted of witchcraft and burned alive at the stake. It was unknown if it was she who bore witness to the book of victims.

The Budapest City Archives, which holds records of the accusations against Elizabeth Bathory, shows that most of the victims were between the ages of 10 to 14, and were commonly burned with hot tongs before being thrown in cold water.

The archived witness statements claim the dead were buried in graveyards around the castle and villages, almost all in unmarked graves. There were even suggestions some of the dead had been buried in the castle itself or burned to ashes.

Due to the Bathory name holding such weight in Hungary at the time, it was believed that a trial and execution would have caused a public scandal. Elizabeth's adult children, and other influential families, claimed the entire hierarchy would be disgraced if she were to be executed.

The initial plan was to make her disappear and embed her with a nunnery in the North of the country but rumours of murderous nobility had taken hold of Hungary, and rebellion was in the air. It was decided that Elizabeth should be placed under house arrest for the rest of her life.

There is a perpetuating legend that Elizabeth was locked into a single windowless room until her death in 1614, but it has recently been suggested she was allowed free movement within the walls of the castle.

Castle arrest, it seemed, would be a better choice of words.

There is one side to Elizabeth's story and legend that is rarely spoken about. That Elizabeth Bathory was no more than a pawn in a game of power to gain a foothold in the Carpathians, and more importantly the strategic position of the Castle of Csejte.

Before Bathory's family and other families intervened, the King wished her executed because it meant he could seize her land – and castle. To have her executed, he needed a story so grim and nasty that execution would be the only desired outcome.

Research shows that many witnesses accounts were based on hearsay, in that they had no first-hand evidence of the tortures and deaths ever taking place. Most servants confessed only under torture by the Hungarian Kingdom, and there exists no document prior to Thurzó's arrival that anyone had complained about Elizabeth at all, which would have been unusual for the time period.

Upon the death of her husband, Elizabeth owned strategically important land, with the castle and villages alone worth an extraordinary amount of wealth. Her wealth and stronghold may have scared the King and he sought to discredit her life before claiming it for himself. It would have been the only way to do it, without enraging the powerful wealthy families in his kingdom.

There is also a suggestion that Elizabeth's husband had been in a huge amount of debt and that Elizabeth refused to sell any of her wealth to settle it, so the Kingdom sought other ways to be rid of her.

The story of Elizabeth Bathory is embedded into popular culture, mystery stories, and true crime tales. But the question remains; was Elizabeth the torturous blood-bathing murderess she has always been made out to be, or someone who was in the way of an ambitious kingdom?

Yet, it is still said the blood of her victims is ingrained into the walls of the Castle of Csejte itself, which can be visited today. Elizabeth was ultimately buried at the Bathory family crypt. When the crypt was opened in 1995 – Elizabeth's body was nowhere to be seen.

Murder at the Tom Tackle Pub

A young woman was brutally attacked and murdered outside a popular Southampton pub, resulting in a 30-year-long miscarriage of justice and the creation of Operation Iceberg.

Southampton on the South Coast of England is famous for its cruise ship harbour, shopping centres, many Universities, and the last port of call for the Mayflower ship that transported English Pilgrims to the New World of America in 1620.

It's also known for murder but you won't find placards about that in the city's museum. One particularly infamous murder took place in 1979, when 22-year-old Teresa Elena De Simone was raped and strangled to death as she got into her car outside the Tom Tackle pub.

What makes this murder so infamous and interesting is that the person ultimately convicted of her murder was innocent and was incarcerated for 27 years before an appeal proved he had not killed her. Instead, it turned out that Teresa had been attacked and killed by a baby-faced 17-year-old boy named David Lace.

Even when he confessed to police he was the murderer, they refused to believe him, and let an innocent man rot in jail for 27 years. Lace's parents were so moved by the murder, they placed an obituary in the local paper that said, '*God only knows why*,' not knowing it was their son who was the culprit.

Teresa was born in 1957 to Mary and Mario de Simone of Italian heritage. When her parents split, her mother married Michael Sedotti and they moved to the residential Shirley area of Southampton, where Teresa grew up in a happy household.

She was known to be a shy but popular girl at school and graduated with good grades that enabled her to get a job as a clerk for the Southern Gas Board, now the British Gas building in the centre of the city, where she worked until her death.

Southampton is also known for its many bars and nightclubs, propped up by the student population that threads through the city. Like any young woman, Teresa had a good social life and was often out drinking in the city on Friday and Saturday nights.

To increase her savings, she took a second part-time evening job at the Tom Tackle pub which was located next to the Mayflower Theatre at the time. Taking the pub job meant that she could broaden her social circle further.

On 4th December 1979, Teresa finished her evening shift at the pub and left with her friend Jenni Savage to go to a local nightclub in the nearby student area of London Road, to celebrate another friend's birthday.

Despite London Road being within walking distance, Jenni decided to drive them both there, and would drop Teresa off to the Tom Tackle car park to collect her own car later on. When they arrived at the club at around 11pm, they had some drinks with friends but decided to leave an hour later.

Jenni drove them back to the Tom Tackle car park where they stayed in the car chatting for about half an hour. Teresa then left to get into her own car. Jenni watched Teresa in the rear-view mirror to see if she got into her car safely, then drove home. It was the last time Teresa was seen alive.

The location of the pub in Commercial Road was only 100 metres from the main Southampton police station and courts of law, which enraged locals when the murder wasn't solved straight away. The following morning, Teresa's mother discovered she had not come home and became concerned.

She and Teresa's stepfather drove to the pub to find Teresa's car still parked up. Believing her to have stayed the night elsewhere, they thought nothing else of it. An hour later, landlord of the Tom Tackle, Anthony Pocock, was expecting a delivery but Teresa's car was blocking the cellar door.

When he went to try and move it himself, he recoiled with horror when he saw Teresa's partially nude body on the back seat. The police arrived within minutes and cornered off the pub, as it was now the scene of a murder.

Teresa was naked from the waist down with her breasts exposed. Her underwear was around her ankles and she had been strangled to death after being raped. A pathologist put the time of death at between 1am and 2am, just a few minutes after Jenni had driven away.

It was suspected that the culprit was either hiding in the shadows watching the two girls, or was waiting in Teresa's car, and made his move when Jenni drove off. The cause of death was strangulation but the pathologist confirmed that due to the white frothy mucous in her mouth, it had been a slow and painful strangulation.

The gold crucifix she was wearing had been taken from her and may have been used as a ligature. It led the local press to label the culprit as the Crucifix Killer, but that moniker didn't last long. Incidentally, the cross was never found.

Despite the murder taking place in the days before DNA profiling, police took swabs, fingerprints and other forensic data which was stored for decades, despite officials claiming it had been destroyed a few years after. The forensic evidence led to the discovery of the real killer 30 years later.

It became one of the largest investigations in Southampton police history. No immediate arrest was made, and in the year that followed, they interviewed approximately 30,000 people, took 2,500 statements and tracked 500 people who had been in the area on the night of the murder. None of which pointed them towards a suspect.

As early as two days after the murder, a man named Sean Hodgson was arrested for stealing from a parked car. He had arrived in Southampton from County Durham two days earlier – the night of the murder. Was it coincidence or something more sinister?

The theft from a vehicle and having arrived in Southampton the night of the murder certainly seemed to point to Hodgson as a suspect. But despite the coincidences, Hodgson's blood type was O and the killer's was A.

Other factors seemed to point away from Hodgson when police received letters from an unidentified writer claiming to know the location and identity of the killer. There were also two anonymous phone calls to Southampton police from a young man claiming to be the killer but they were not taken seriously.

On 16th May 1980, Hodgson pleaded guilty to theft from a vehicle and was granted bail awaiting sentencing. When he was arrested in London on a similar offence a month later, he was sentenced to three years in prison, where he confessed to multiple crimes as a way of bolstering his image in prison, many of which were untrue.

A year after the murder, almost to the day, Hodgson confessed to a priest that he had killed a woman near the Tom Tackle pub in Southampton. Hodgson was escorted from prison to the car park of the Tom Tackle, where it was written he gave details about the case that only the killer could have known.

That Hodgson turned out to be innocent was something of an oddity, he had spent time in a psychiatric hospital before moving to Southampton, and his delusions may have been playing with him. It was also suspected police fed him some of the unreleased details of the murder so that they could finally pin it on someone.

At the same time, he also confessed to two other murders, both of which turned out to be untrue and had never taken place. At the trial, he confessed to being a pathological liar due to his mental condition and confessed to unsolved crimes he didn't commit because he wanted someone to pay for them.

The prosecution posited a story that Hodgson had got drunk, fell asleep in Teresa's car, which was unlocked, and then attacked her when she entered the vehicle. In February 1982, Hodgson was found guilty of murder and sentenced to life in prison.

He was denied parole multiple times for continuously claiming he was innocent, something that would pose a risk if an offender was released. 26 years later, in 2008, Hodgson contacted London solicitors, Julian Young and Co. who specialised in bringing appeals against convictions.

The lead solicitor, Rag Chand, spent four months attempting to trace the forensic evidence from the scene of the murder, but was constantly told it had been destroyed in 1998 in accordance with best practices.

Unwilling to give in and going with a gut feeling that something was untoward, Chand was directed to an evidence archive on an industrial estate in the Midlands, which appeared to be unused and unprotected. It was there, he found the forensic evidence he needed.

In early 2009, after DNA analysis of the semen swab, it was confirmed that they did not come from Hodgson, which meant he was not the killer and was innocent. The only crime he had committed was a theft from a vehicle and multiple confessions due to his mental capability.

In February 2009, after 27 years in prison as an innocent man, Hodgson was released to public fanfare – and disgust at the system that had kept him captive for most of his life. Prior to his release, Hodgson had been diagnosed with schizophrenia and depression. He received a paltry £250,000 in compensation.

He received no care after his release and a year later was in court again over allegations of rape and sexual assault of a woman with learning difficulties.

He was sentenced to a community order that involved intense psychiatric care.

In 2012, just three years after his release, Hodgson died of emphysema, a smoking-related disease. But two big questions remained; who had killed Teresa and where was he hiding?

A month after Hodgson had been released, and armed with forensic evidence, police reopened the Teresa murder case and called it Operation Iceberg, assumed to be because of the length of time the case had been truly unsolved, and as cold as a cold case could get.

No matches were found in a search of the DNA database but police pressed on to test as many of the original suspects as possible and spent many months going through old statements and papers relating to the case.

Half a year later, genetic familial testing discovered a possible link to a suspect. A sibling of a man named David Lace was found to have a partial match to the DNA they had on record. Unfortunately for the investigation, Lace had taken his own life in 1988 for reasons then unknown.

In the summer of 2009, Lace's body was exhumed in a cemetery in neighbouring city Portsmouth and it was confirmed that the forensic evidence matched Lace. It would have been a billion-to-one chance for it to be someone else.

Then police uncovered what they already suspected but feared wasn't true. Lace had already confessed he was the killer to police back in 1983 while in custody on unrelated charges. But because Hodgson had been convicted of the murder, the police ignored it.

It was also suggested but never confirmed that Lace was the person who had phoned the police station and sent the letters in the days following the murder. He had been arrested in 1980 and charged with theft. When he committed more burglaries while on probation, he was arrested again and sentenced to five years in prison.

Lace was released from Dartmoor prison in 1987, and less than a year later took his own life without an obvious motive. It's clear now that he couldn't cope with the guilt of what he had done and that an innocent man had gone to jail instead of him.

His family claimed he had become depressed since his release, gave away his possessions, apologised to them for his past actions, and resigned from his new job – all signs of suicidal ideation. He was found dead by his landlord on 9th December 1988, just over nine years to the day that he had killed Teresa.

In his statement to police back in 1983, Lace said that he was outside the Tom Tackle pub when Jenni dropped Teresa back to her car. When Teresa got into her car, he knocked on the window then forced his way in, locking the doors behind him.

He described how he raped her and strangled her using the seatbelt of the passenger seat. He then stole her handbag and jewellery to make it look like a robbery. He hid in the shadows for ten minutes before catching a train back to Portsmouth where he lived at the time.

But police didn't believe him because they thought the real killer was already in jail. As a result of the case, new laws were introduced that meant all evidence would remain accessible until a convicted person was released, something which would have led to Hodgson's release many years earlier.

It was a bittersweet ending to a case that had let an innocent man rot in jail for almost 30 years, left a promising young woman dead, and a suicide with dark secrets that were taken to the grave.

Murder at the Metropolitan Opera

A violinist playing for the Metropolitan Opera vanished during the intermission only to be found murdered the following morning by a killer the media had dubbed The Phantom of the Opera.

The Metropolitan Opera (the Met) was founded in 1883 on Broadway and moved to the Lincoln Center site in 1966. By then it had become the largest classical music organisation in North America. To play in the orchestra there was to have reached the pinnacle of one's career.

On 23rd July 1980, the Berlin Ballet were being hosted by the Met with guest dancers Galina Panov, Valery Panov, and Rudolf Nureyev. The auditorium was sold out and the music filled the building. For violinist Thomas Suarez, it was a dream come true.

During the first piece of music, the Firebird, he was sitting behind 31-year-old violinist Helen Hagnes, a friend and regular with the orchestra. When they broke for an interval, Suarez headed to the canteen and chatted with other musicians about the opening acts, over a cup of hot coffee.

When the orchestra returned to the pit to play Don Quixote, Suarez noticed that Helen had not returned from the interval. It was not uncommon for one of the orchestra to be late back to the pit but everyone normally returned before the curtains rose.

However, as the seconds passed, Suarez and other members of the orchestra were becoming concerned. The lights dimmed and the curtain lifted but there was no sign of Helen. Assuming she had become ill, Suarez put Helen's violin in her case and placed it on the floor.

When the ballet ended for the night, Helen was nowhere to be seen and her violin remained beside her seat. Suarez returned home to his apartment on the same street where Helen lived but she had not returned home.

The following morning, reports were coming in of a body discovered in the Metropolitan Opera. It appeared that Helen never left the opera house. She had been stripped, gagged, and thrown from the roof into a six-storey air shaft.

Helen was raised on a chicken farm in Aldergrove, British Columbia, with three sisters. Her Swedish parents emigrated from Finland in the mid-1950s to give their children a better education. Between the ages of 8 to 19, Helen was supported by her parents to play the violin.

Despite living off meagre funds themselves, they poured all they could into providing a better life for her and the music. And so it was that Helen grew up with a dream to be part of one of the greatest musical organisations in America – The Met Opera Orchestra.

Along the way, she became first violinist for the Seattle Symphony Orchestra, and later got a scholarship at the famous Julliard school for performing arts in New York City. Before she landed the big seat at the Met, she married a sculptor named Janis Mintiks, the love of her life.

While training to master the violin, Helen studied in Italy and Switzerland, and performed on cruise ships between America and Europe. It was on the ships where she met her best friend, pianist Judith Olsen. Together they played music on the high seas and dreamt of playing for the big time orchestras.

On one voyage as they approached Egypt, Helen told Judith of her beliefs in reincarnation. She believed Egypt to be her ancient home and she felt at peace in the country. She made her husband promise to bring her ashes to Egypt if anything were to happen to her.

Except, her husband never truly believed that Helen would die before him.

On the night of the Berlin Ballet, Helen had left the violin on the seat to get a drink at the interval. The Met was known to have been a fortress with some of the highest levels of security of any public building in New York. If anything was to happen, it would have come from the inside.

In a backstage elevator, Helen was headed to the auditorium when a man followed her in and closed the door. He was 21-year-old Craig Crimmins, a stagehand with an unsavoury appetite for pretty women from the orchestra.

Born in the Bronx, Crimmins was raised an Irish Catholic and grew up with boyish looks and an immature outlook. Crimmins was stoned and drunk and smelled of booze. It was a relief when the doors opened so that Helen could escape the smell of the elevator.

As she stepped out, Crimmins grabbed her shoulder and asked her for sexual services. Enraged by his actions, Helen slapped him. Crimmins walked after her and asked her for sex again but Helen pushed him away.

Suddenly, Crimmins lost control and hit her in the back of the head, continuing to beat her as she fell to the ground. Realising no-one was around, he dragged her to a stairwell and started ripping off her clothes with the intention of raping her.

When he failed to perform the act, he tied Helen up and marched her to the roof of the building and attempted to rape her again. When that failed, he stood her up and kicked her down the Met's air shaft, an open ventilation courtyard on the side of the building.

Helen's body was discovered the morning after the murder and stirred up public imagination with many news outlets running with the 'Phantom of the Opera Murder'. Every single person in the building on the night of the murder was questioned.

This included Crimmins who lied about his whereabouts. To the investigation, this meant that of the hundreds of people at the ballet that night, no-one had seen Helen at the interval. The

Phantom story grew stronger with each passing day.

Helen's friends and previous boyfriends were questioned but the security continued to claim the Met was impenetrable during showtimes. A month passed until police decided to question everyone again. This time, Crimmins broke down and confessed to the attempted rape and murder.

One year later, Crimmins was sentenced to 20 years to life in prison and went down with the moniker of the Phantom of the Opera.

Despite the murder, the orchestra had to reconvene on the night of the discovery and play to a packed audience. For Thomas Suarez, the murder was at the forefront of his mind when he played with the orchestra for Valery Panov's Ballet 'The Idiot'.

The ballet's first terrifying notes, taken from Shostakovich's symphonies, sent a chill through the numbed orchestra. In the third act of the ballet, after the interval, the heroine, Nastasya Filippovna, is found murdered. It was as if art had imitated real life.

For Janis, the loss of his wife was too much to bear but he had made a promise to take her ashes to Egypt, to connect with her ancient home. Unsure how to do it and realising he needed more funds and knowledge, Janis wrote a letter to the Egyptian president Anwar Sadat.

Happily, Sadat replied, and Egypt arranged flights for Janis and Helen's ashes. Helen's wish was fulfilled and she finally found peace in the country of her dreams.

Dennis Nilsen: Serial Killer

The sickening tale of British serial killer Dennis Nilsen, who killed 15 young men, and dissected some of their remains – before flushing them down the toilet and blocking the sewers with flesh.

Dennis Nilsen is one of Britain's most infamous serial killers. Some see him as the British version of Jeffrey Dahmer and in a lot of ways, the similarities are striking. They both killed gay men and they made their first kill within five months of each other in 1978. Nilsen killed 15, Dahmer killed 17, and they both carried out necrophilia acts upon the bodies of their victims.

Yet, the very nature of their crimes are inherently different. Because of the United Kingdom's different legal system to that of the United States,

Dennis Nilsen was sentenced to life, as since 1969, the country no longer carries the death sentence.

Nilsen would request parole hearings for immediate release up until his death in 2018 when he died of natural causes. He reached out from within his cell with now banned autobiographies and interviews to sate the appetite of the curious public.

He murdered 15 young men in London over a five year period and kept the victims' bodies for a certain amount of time after he had killed. Then he dissected them and either burned the remains or flushed them down the toilet.

In his life he worked as a military chef, police officer and civil servant. Not the usual career progression to serial killer. To stand in such esteemed positions in work and life and then go on to kill is one that has produced conflicting reports from psychologists and experts alike.

His early life consisted of his parents divorcing because of his father becoming an alcoholic. Nilsen was only four-years-old when it happened and his mother remarried soon afterwards. The disruption in the British Isles after the dust of World War Two had settled was felt throughout the nation, more so on the children born into that era.

The fallout of World War Two across many countries is considered one of the reasons for the rise of the serial killer in the Seventies and Eighties. For Nilsen, the break-up of his family at a time of national hardship was crippling.

In his trial and subsequent interviews, Nilsen claimed there was an event in his life, at the age of six-years-old, that was to shape him for many years to come. After his mother remarried, she sent him to live with his grandparents.

It was there that he found a kinship with his grandfather, Andrew Whyte, but after a couple of years he was returned to his mother in 1951. In the Autumn of that year, Nilsen's grandfather died of a heart attack.

Some serial killers have attributed the death of a grandparent as a turning point in their lives. Alexander Pichushkin, the Russian Chessboard Killer, confirmed that after the death of his grandfather he turned to vodka, and then to murder.

What didn't help Nilsen's fragile tendencies at the time was that his mother made him view the body of his grandfather due to her strong religious beliefs. Some psychologists have suggested this was one of the markers that put Nilsen onto a different path.

He later stated that the first time he knew of his grandfather's death was when he saw the corpse. *"It caused a sort of emotional death inside me."* – Dennis Nilsen

Two years later, when he was eight-years-old, Nilsen almost drowned in the seas close to his hometown. An older boy who was on the coast at the time saw what was happening and went in to rescue him. Nilsen later claimed that the boy masturbated over his body. He awoke from his experience with near death to find ejaculate on his stomach.

Afterwards, he withdrew into himself, hiding away from the world. He was a loner and kept himself to himself but he was never disliked and had many friends at the time. Yet, he preferred to be with his own company.

He had never killed small animals or exhibited a cruel streak towards living things. He was never aggressive or violent towards his peers. He was for all intents and purposes, a good and well-loved child, and the opposite of what a potential serial killer was supposed to have been.

On one occasion he helped in the search of a local man who had gone missing. As fate would have it, it was a young Nilsen and a friend who found the man's body on a riverbank. He later said it had reminded him of seeing the body of his grandfather and upon coming across the corpse he had felt no emotion towards it.

He never had a sexual encounter, nor suffered abuse during his childhood or teenage years. It would be almost two decades later when Nilsen would record his first kill.

He joined the British Army at 17-years-old and stayed there for 11 years. During his military years he said he carried with him a huge weight of loneliness. When he was allowed a private room he would lay down in front of a mirror so he couldn't see his own head in the reflection. He would then masturbate to the sight of what he felt was an unconscious body.

This might in some part have been carried over from his experience on the beach. In 1972 he left the military of his own accord and returned to civilian life. He went on to join the Metropolitan Police in London but only served eight months as an officer before once again leaving of his own accord.

He often witnessed autopsied bodies in close proximity. It fascinated him and he revelled in that part of the job but he left because he felt the job didn't fit him well, having come from the military. In 1974 he went on to work as a civil servant in a job centre in London and became active in trade unions. Then the fantasies he'd long held started to seep into his reality.

There are infamous addresses where killers and murderers have carried out their crimes and lived but none more so than 195 Melrose Avenue. The address in the London area of Cricklewood, would claim 12 victims. He had access to a large garden and was able to burn many of the remains in bonfires. Some of the entrails were thrown over the fence so that local wildlife would consume them.

Nilsen moved into 195 Melrose Avenue, sometimes listed mistakenly as Melrose Place, with a man named David Gallichan. It was said to have been purely a platonic relationship. Nilsen wanted more however, he wanted real commitment and after a series of casual sexual encounters, his bizarre corpse fantasies started to become more prominent.

When he positioned himself in front of a mirror so that his head appeared as missing, he would start to add fake blood to his corpse to look as though he had been killed. He fantasised someone would take him away and bury him and he started to believe that his corpse was the perfect state of his human body.

There was nothing more emotionally and physically pleasing to him than fantasising about his own dead body. After a rough and stressful relationship with Gallichan, Nilsen forced him to leave but was aware of the consequences of being alone. "*Loneliness,*" he wrote, "*is a long unbearable pain.*"

A day before New Year's Eve, in 1978, Nilsen took his first victim. 14-year-old Stephen Holmes had been refused alcohol at a local pub. Nilsen took the opportunity to invite him to his flat on Melrose Avenue to drink alcohol with him. "*He was to stay with me over the New Year period whether he wanted to or not.*"

After going to bed together, Nilsen woke at dawn and became aroused at the sight of his new friend's sleeping body. Holmes was sleeping on his front when Nilsen straddled him and slipped a tie under his neck. He subsequently drowned the young boy in a bucket of water by resting his head over the edge of a chair.

After the bubbles stopped rising from the water, Nilsen rested him on the floor realising that he had just killed a man whose name he did not know. He was also suddenly fearful of the conscquences of his actions. Again, a trait not carried by most serial killers.

Nilsen said later that he just sat there staring at the boy's fresh corpse, shaking with the fear and stress of the situation. He made himself a coffee and smoked some cigarettes to ease his nerves.

After washing the corpse in the bathroom he returned Holmes to the bed and was fascinated by the limpness of the corpse. *"It was the beginning of the end of my life as I had known it, I had started down the avenue of death and possession of a new kind of flat-mate."*

The concept of keeping corpses as flat-mates was now embedded into Nilsen's psyche. He thought the sight of the corpse was beautiful and not appalling in anyway whatsoever. He hid the body under the floorboards, but after a week had gone by, curiosity had got the better of him – he wanted to see whether the body had changed in anyway.

As he was carrying the body back to the living room, he felt himself becoming aroused and subsequently masturbated onto the corpse's stomach. He even trussed him up by the ankles for an undisclosed amount of time before putting the corpse back under the floorboards.

It would be almost eight months later when Nilsen removed the body to burn it in a bonfire in his garden. He burned rubber to hide the smell and raked the ashes into his garden. Most of his victims were homeless or homosexual men who he would lure to his home with offers of food, alcohol or a place to rest their heads.

His victims were normally killed by strangulation or drowning during the course of the night. He then proceeded to use his butchering skills, learned in the British Army, to help him get rid of the bodies.

He would keep them in various different locations around his home but usually under the floorboards and would constantly engage in sexual activity with the corpses. Over the next three years, Nilsen would murder another 11 men in the ground floor apartment at Melrose Avenue. Of these 11, only four were ever identified.

Kenneth Ockendon was a Canadian tourist he had met at a local pub for lunch in 1979. Nilsen claimed he enjoyed the company of Ockendon and it was the thought of him leaving that drove him to kill again. He strangled him with a headphone cord before washing the body and taking it to bed with him.

Nilsen said he never had sexual intercourse with the corpses but that he did carry out sexual acts with them. He enjoyed masturbating on the corpses and pleasuring himself on certain parts of their bodies. He placed Ockendon under the floorboards and would take the corpse out several times to watch the television with him.

Nilsen said he would sometimes go into a killing trance and didn't always remember the act of murder. The feeling of control over the corpses of his flat-mates thrilled him and he held a certain fascination with how their corpses deteriorated over time. He believed he was appreciating them more dead than alive.

When the investigation started after Nilsen's arrest, police investigators found over 1000 bone fragments in the garden of 195 Melrose Avenue. He had used the small garden as his own personal burial ground.

Through his butchering career in the British Army he learned the art of butchery so well he would use this skill to rid the house piece by piece of the corpses that remained. He would strip to his underwear and cut them up on the stone floor of his kitchen. He would then place the organs in a plastic bag.

His fantasy progressed to removing the head and then heating it in a large pan of water to boil off the flesh of the skull. He would burn the rest of the remains over time, sometimes close to the garden fence. He was constantly amazed that he was never caught or that no one ever questioned him and his strange activities.

Nilsen one day decided to leave Melrose Avenue and move into a new place in the city. In some part to leave the murderous part of his life behind and in others to escape from the torment he had inflicted. Before Fred and Rose West's 25 Cromwell Street was known to the public, 195 Melrose Avenue was the darkest house of horrors in the British Isles.

In 1981, Nilsen moved to 23 Cranley Gardens and it proved to be his undoing. He found it difficult to get rid of the bodies in his new home and ended up with black bin-liners full of human organs in his wardrobe. He would kill three more at Cranley Gardens over the coming year and a half.

The last victim was dissected in the same way as the previous ones. The head was boiled and the limbs and organs were placed into bags, ready for disposal. But without access to a garden, Nilsen had to come up with different methods of disposal.

He would boil the flesh off the bones and start flushing pieces of the bodies down the toilet.

One of the other five tenants who lived in the block complained to the landlord the toilet was not flushing properly. Nilsen had apparently tried to clear the blockage with acid and it mostly worked but it didn't clear the blockage in the external drain.

A local plumber called in a specialist team to get a second opinion and 48 hours later they arrived. One of the technicians, Michael Cattran, went into the drains beneath the house. He found a gooey sludge blocking a part of the sewer coming from a pipe linked to the house.

It appeared to be various pieces of animal flesh and so he immediately reported it to his superiors. When the sewer team left, Nilsen went down into the sewers and started removing the lumps of flesh that had congealed together. But some of the other tenants noticed his movements and strange actions and reported it to the police.

At the same time, the results came back from the analysis of what was assumed to be animal remains. The results were unquestionable; it was human remains. Detectives paid a visit to the house the following evening.

DCI Peter Jay waited at the scene with two officers for Nilsen to return from work, they followed him into the block of flats and they immediately smelled rotting flesh. Nilsen asked why the police were interested in the drains. They told him they had found human remains.

"Good grief, how awful," Nilsen said.

"Don't mess about, son, where's the rest of the body?" DCI Jay responded.

Nilsen remained relaxed and calmly said that the remains of the bodies were in two plastic bags in the wardrobe. When they drove him to the police station, they asked him how many bodies he was actually talking about.

"Fifteen or sixteen since 1978."

He pleaded guilty with diminished responsibility but on November 4th, 1983, he was sentenced to life imprisonment. He was convicted of six murders and two attempted murders. The Home Secretary later imposed a whole life tariff, which meant that he would never be released and would subsequently be denied any requests for parole.

Nilsen died of natural causes in 2018. His disturbing crimes have been made into various movies, TV series, multiple books, and thousands of articles, each trying to uncover the madness behind the eyes of one of Britain's worst serial killers.

The Evil Kingdom of Ervil LeBaron

A polygamous cult leader ordered the murders of at least 25 people, many from beyond the grave, in a tale of fear, control, and a mission to create the Kingdom of God on Earth.

Children of cult leader Ervil LeBaron claimed they were taught to live in awe of their father as he was a self-proclaimed prophet of God and the one true prophet on Earth. They were taught that they were celestial children, whose destinies were to follow in Ervil's footsteps.

Except, not all was peachy in Ervil's church. Many of his wives were married to him when they were underage, and he was known to abuse his children and other members of the group. He also ordered mob-style hits against his rivals or those who stood against his cult.

The *Church of Jesus Christ of Latter-day Saints* (Mormon Church) banned polygamy (more than one spouse at the same time) in 1890 but has been tarnished with the trait ever since as they never entirely removed it from their doctrine.

At that time, those Mormons who believed polygamy was their right, split from the church and moved to Mexico to avoid U.S. Law. In 1924, Alma LeBaron Sr., who believed in polygamy, moved his two wives and eight children to North Mexico where he started a farm and commune called Colonia LeBaron.

When Alma died in 1951, leadership was transferred to his son Joel LeBaron. Joel was able to circumnavigate U.S. law and incorporated the community as the *Church of the Firstborn of the Fulness of Times* in Utah.

His younger brother, Ervil LeBaron, was second in command for a short time and split his time between the Utah group and the new Baja Peninsula group; Los Molinos. In the late 1960s, Ervil fought for control of the group, leading to membership of the group splitting into two factions.

God then apparently ordered Ervil to split from his brother's leadership and form his own church in San Diego called the *Church of the First Born of the*

Lamb of God. It was then that God apparently told Ervil to start killing people.

On August 20th 1972, Ervil ordered his followers to head back down to Mexico and kill Joel, as God had told him to do so. Two followers carried out his wishes and killed Joel by beating and shooting him. Two years later, in Mexico, Ervil was tried and convicted of Joel's murder but an appeal overturned his conviction on a technicality – though some suspect the courts were bribed.

Joel's death was the first in a long line of murders and crimes associated with Ervil's cult. In retaliation for Ervil having gone to trial, his followers descended on Los Molinos and destroyed the commune, killing two more men in the process.

Realising he could gain more power – or on the word of God, as he put it – Ervil turned his attention to Mormon leaders of other groups who held polygamous views. In April 1975, minster Bob Simons, known for teaching Native Americans, was killed on Ervil's orders.

In 1977, Ervil ordered his 13th wife and her daughter to kill leader of the *Apostolic United Brethren*, Rulon C. Allred. They killed him without question and later claimed in a book that Ervil was using mind control and fear to keep his followers loyal.

Ervil turned his attention to killing his own family members whenever they showed intentions to leave his cult. He ordered his 10th wife, Vonda White, to kill follower Dean Glover, as he had attempted to leave. Vonda was later sentenced to life in prison for the murder, in addition to being suspected of another killing.

The self-proclaimed prophet of God also ordered the murder of his own 17-year-old pregnant daughter, Rebecca LeBaron, as she asked if she could leave the group to raise her second child. But if the murders were bad enough, it was made worse when Ervil began ordering kills from behind bars – and beyond the grave.

The church moved around to avoid detection from the law and split their time between the U.S. and Mexico. But the law was already onto the cult. Ervil was arrested in 1979 and ultimately sentenced to life in prison in 1980 for ordering the death of Rulon Allred.

Despite his conviction, his remaining followers still believed he was the one true prophet on Earth and waited for instructions. While in prison, Ervil wrote a new bible called *The Book of the New Covenants*, which contained a commandment ordering followers to kill those who wish to leave or didn't follow orders.

20 copies of the bible were printed and distributed among his followers. Little did the prison guards know that inside the bible was a list of names of people that Ervil claimed had gone against God and his cult and needed to be killed.

Ervil died of apparent natural causes in the summer of 1981 but his followers were still active. Two days after his death, Verlan LeBaron died in a suspicious car accident in Mexico City. Seven years later, in 1988, the cult struck again.

At exactly 4pm on June 27th 1988, four murders were committed simultaneously in Texas. One of Ervil's former followers, Duane Chynoweth, who had escaped the cult many years earlier, was shot dead with his eight-year-old daughter as they ran errands.

Ervil's stepson, Eddie Marston, was killed as he walked down a local street. And at the same time, father of six Mark Chynoweth was shot multiple times as he sat in his office in downtown Houston. It appeared that Ervil had the power to order murders from beyond the grave.

The Texas murders became known as the 4 O'clock Murders, and over the next two decades, five people were convicted of them, including one of Ervil's daughters. Much of the testimony and documents given during the LeBaron trials were sealed by the courts.

The Book of the New Covenants has never been publicly released but some members of the LeBaron family had it digitized many years ago. Some of Ervil's children carried on his teachings claiming that his way was the right way, and that it was their mission to establish the Kingdom of God on Earth.

Some of the dead have never been accounted for and additional victims linked to the LeBaron cult continue to appear. In 1989, six of Ervil's children left various foster homes at the same time in an organised escape and were suspected to have rejoined the cult in Mexico, with rumours a refuge still exists somewhere in the country.

In 2017, one of Ervil's daughters, Anna LeBaron, told her story to the BBC. She told how the cult would move from one safehouse to the next and that they slept on filthy floors and lived off food that had been thrown away by nearby residents.

She explained how Ervil had all of them under a grip of terror and that they would have to do everything he asked for fear of being murdered. He taught them that the outside world didn't understand them which is why they had to keep moving around to avoid the law.

The young children of the cult were beaten for showing any sign of attitude or anger towards Ervil. Female marriage age in the LeBaron family was set at 15 but came with allowances to marry younger girls should they be the right fit. Ervil was known to have married some of his wives at such a young age.

An estimated 25 to 30 people were murdered on the orders of Ervil LeBaron, whether in person or posthumously, and his cult legacy continues to be felt today. In the land of cults, the LeBaron family sit head and shoulders above the rest, leading some elements of the media to have labelled Ervil as the Mormon Manson.

Devil-Worshipping Camden Ripper

A devil-worshipping serial killer brutally murdered and dismembered at least three sex workers before dumping their body parts in canals and bins around Camden.

Camden, England, is nothing if not the epicentre of a world's worth of bonkers and varied lifestyles, I should know, I live there. As with many London boroughs, crime exists, sometimes obviously, other times not so much, but there is always the feeling that the nights are considered riskier than the day.

Beyond the world food stalls, crowds of visitors, alternative fashion, and labyrinthine markets, there exists a town that's earned its worth as one of London's most popular areas. But throw a serial killer into the mix, and Camden is pushed to the edge.

Born in 1951, Anthony John Hardy became known as the Camden Ripper, for the murders of three women in 2002. It was an unusual case, as his lifestyle and age didn't fit the profile the police had drawn up to catch him, as he claimed his first convicted victim when he was 51-years-old.

He grew up in Burton-upon-Trent in Staffordshire to a hard-working family and allegedly had a good childhood with no indication of what was to come. After earning good school grades, he enrolled at the illustrious Imperial College London where he graduated with a degree in engineering.

While studying for his degree, he met his future wife Judith Dwight, who he married in 1972. Over the next few years, Hardy became the manager of a large company and had three sons and one daughter with Judith.

Due to his work, he moved the family to Tasmania, Australia, where the children were raised. But from 1982, Hardy began to change, and there was no obvious moment when it happened. He was known to have displayed symptoms of mental illness but wasn't diagnosed with anything at the time.

In fact, Hardy's case sits very much in the nurture camp of the nurture vs. nature debate, in that he turned to the dark side in his thirties, finding a passion for devil worship and a kinship with none other than Jack the Ripper.

While in Tasmania in 1982, Hardy attacked Judith. He filled a water bottle and froze it before using it to hit Judith over the head as she slept. He then dragged her unconscious body to the bathtub where he attempted to drown her. Fortunately, she awoke and managed to fight him off.

Judith didn't press charges but Hardy agreed to check himself into a psychiatric hospital in Queensland, where he stayed for a month before being placed under mental health care. Following on from that, he ended up stalking Judith for a couple of years and told a psychiatrist that he wanted to kill her.

In 1985, Hardy left his family in Australia and returned to the UK. In 1986, Judith was successful in obtaining a divorce from him because of the stalking and worrying behaviour. She also gained custody of their children and remained in Australia, which sent Hardy on a downward spiral.

Over the next few years, Hardy was in and out of psychiatric hospitals and mental health care and diagnosed with depression and bipolar disorder. He quickly turned to drink and drugs as a way to cope with his life.

When he was a child, he promised himself that he would escape his working class roots and become someone better than the life he was given. And for a while, being manager of a company and a growing family, he lived his promise. But the divorce left him on the bread line with no job and family, and so Hardy developed a hatred not only of himself, but the world around him.

He was admitted to various hospitals for alcohol abuse and was often found in a drug-induced psychosis, where he couldn't remember his own name. He lived in various hostels around London due to being homeless a lot of the time, before getting a council flat on a quiet Camden estate, at Number 4 Hartland, Royal College Street.

Throughout the 1990s, and in his forties, he began using sex workers from money he had made selling on stolen goods. He was arrested multiple times for theft but got away with a prison term each time due to his deteriorating mental health.

In 1998, Hardy was arrested when a sex worker accused him of raping her. Police investigated the incident but concluded there was not enough evidence to charge Hardy, who yet again, was admitted to a psychiatric hospital.

Many of Hardy's neighbours later spoke of his strange behaviour and that he acted strange around other people and was argumentative, especially when it came to communal areas. He was once found in the bin area sitting on the floor, hitting a hammer on the ground for no apparent reason. He was also spotted going through neighbours bins and taking some of their rubbish back into his flat.

What police didn't know at the time but were later made aware of was that Hardy was discharged from a London psychiatric hospital just days before he claimed his first victim. Though convicted of three murders, Hardy was positively linked to two more.

On 17th December 2000, a man walking along the River Thames near Battersea, spotted something unusual in the water at the side of the riverbank. He moved in for a closer look and realised it was the upper body of a female, who had been severed at the waist.

Medical examiners concluded she had been in the water for at least two weeks and had been sliced in half with a sword or machete. She was later identified through tattoo recognition as 24-year-old sex worker Zoe Louise Parker.

In late February 2001, three young boys were fishing along the Regent's Canal in Camden when they dragged up a heavy bag from the sludge that had been weighed down with bricks. Inside, they found the remains of various body parts belonging to 31-year-old sex worker and mother of two Paula Fields from Liverpool who had been dismembered with a hacksaw.

With two horrific murders on their hands, police were quick to shut down rumours of a serial killer, but that's exactly what they had on their hands. Paula's boyfriend became the first suspect but there was no evidence against him. Police suggested that the killer had either kept the other parts of her body as a trophy or that there were more body parts in bags throughout the Regent's Canal.

In January 2002, one of Hardy's neighbours called police as she suspected Hardy had vandalised her front door and poured acid through the letter box. When police entered Hardy's flat, they found a locked door but Hardy claimed he didn't have a key to it.

Police broke the door down and found the body of a naked dead woman on his bed, covered in cuts and bruises. She was later identified as 38-year-old sex worker Sally White who had been seen with Hardy the night before.

Hardy claimed to have no recollection of how Sally had come to be in his bed, due to his alcohol dependency and mental health issues. While police decided what to do with Hardy, he was transferred to yet another psychiatric hospital where he stayed for 11 months until late November 2002 – just days before the next murder and was allowed to return to his old flat.

Amazingly, the forensic pathologist in the case of Sally White concluded she had died of a heart attack, despite the wounds that Hardy inflicted upon her – which was the sole reason Hardy wasn't charged with Sally's murder. The pathologist would later be struck off the General Medical Council.

On 30th December, a homeless person was rummaging for food in a Camden bin when he found a black bag containing various body parts. The two women were later identified as 29-year-old Elizabeth Selina Valad and 34-year-old Brigitte MacClennan. Both women were sex workers in and around Camden. Brigitte was ultimately identified through DNA and Elizabeth was identified via the serial number on her breast implants.

A double murder enquiry was launched but police didn't have to look far as Hardy was already on their radar. Investigators found eight more bags containing body parts close to where the first bag had been found. Brigitte's torso was found in a wheelie bin less than 100 metres away.

Hardy's flat was only a few hundred metres from where the body parts had been dumped, which made it easy for police to discover who the suspect was, as they literally followed a trail of blood to Hardy's flat. They obtained a warrant and entered the property but Hardy was nowhere to be seen.

However, the evidence was overwhelming. There was a hacksaw on the kitchen worktop with human skin still attached to it, along with an electric jigsaw power tool, women's shoes and porn magazines everywhere they looked.

A large amount of blood and blood splatter was found in the bathroom with a devil's mask beside the bath, which was worn by Hardy when he killed and cut up his victims. A note on a table in the living room read 'Sally White RIP.'

Satanic messages were written in blood on the walls of the flat along with blood stains on the floor and ceiling. Then police found a number of black bags in the closet containing more body parts, and the torso of Elizabeth. It was suspected that Hardy had sex with the corpses of his victims.

A large search to hunt Hardy got underway but it was suspected he had fled the area. Three days later on New Year's Day 2003, he was spotted by an off-duty policeman filling in a prescription for his diabetic mediation at University College Hospital.

After a longer than usual wait, Hardy walked outside and attempted to hide behind some bins but two officers approached and got into a fight with him. One was knocked unconscious and the other was stabbed through the hand and had his eye dislocated from his socket. The injured officer was still able to restrain Hardy before back-up arrived and he was finally arrested.

Both Brigitte's and Elizabeth heads and hands were never found and are suspected to either be at the bottom of the Regent's canal or had unknowingly been taken to a waste disposal facility. Another sex worker came forward and said she had been invited back to Hardy's flat around the time of the murders, meaning that Hardy hoped to kill as many as he could.

Following Hardy's arrest, and in the years that followed, there was public outcry as to how Hardy was allowed to kill after being released from mental health care multiple times and not being charged with Sally's murder. Had he been kept in hospital or charged with Sally's murder, then at least two more women would still be alive today.

Hardy pleaded guilty to three counts of murder and was ultimately sentenced to life in prison. He was imprisoned at the specialist Dangerous and Severe Personality Disorder (DSPD) unit at

Frankland Prison in County Durham, where he died of sepsis on 26th November 2020, aged 69.

It is strongly believed that Hardy also killed Zoe Louise Parker and Paula Fields. In recent years, he has also been connected to the murders of sex workers Sharon Hoare in 1991 and Christine McGovern in 1995. All four additional murders remain unsolved to this day. If Hardy did kill them, which investigators believe he did, then he could have murdered seven women in total and may be one of Britain's worst serial killers.

Charlie Chop-off

A serial killer in New York gained the name of Charlie Chop-off, for attacking young boys and mutilating their genitals, in an urban legend born from real life.

In different areas of Manhattan during the early 1970s, young black boys were being attacked and left for dead. The killer mutilated their genitals and either chopped off their penis and left it on the body or took it with him.

A man named Erno Soto, sometimes referred to as Miguel Rivera, was held as a suspect. Despite the killer being caught and linked to two of the murders, the case remains open, as he was unfit to stand trial.

The attacks and murders took place between March 1972 and May 1974 in and around Manhattan. The first murder took place on 9th March when eight-year-old Douglas Owens was found on the rooftop of an apartment block in Harlem.

An autopsy showed he had been stabbed 38 times in his chest and neck, and his penis had been sliced in two. Friends and family were questioned but to no avail. The killer had managed to lure the boy to the top of the building without being seen or heard.

Already, the murder turned heads. The locals began asking questions. Who could have done this to such a young boy? Why had they done it? Was the killer likely to strike again? And more importantly, was the killer hiding among them?

As the investigation into Owen's murder stagnated, another attack shocked the region. Six weeks after the murder, an unidentified 10-year-old black boy was lured into an apartment building on the West Side. He was raped, stabbed, had his penis removed, and left for dead.

Miraculously, the boy survived, and was able to give a partial description of the man. His attacker was a thin, tall man who had medium dark sink and a mole on his left cheek but the details were not good enough for an artist's sketch. The boy's penis was later found in a park in Manhattan.

Due to the genital mutilation, the murder of Owens and the attack on the boy were linked to the same culprit. However, some investigators claimed the link was tentative, despite the obvious similarities. It took another two victims for police to be certain there was a serial killer in the city.

A few months passed with no new attack until 23rd October 1972 when nine-year-old Wendell Hubbard was killed in East Harlem. Wendell's mother had seen him in the yard of the home only an hour beforehand. When she called him up for dinner, she realised he had gone missing.

Due to the previous attacks, she contacted the police right away. Less than four hours later, his body was found by three boys playing on the roof of an apartment building, only six blocks from the Owens murder.

Wendell had been stabbed 17 times in the neck and chest, and his penis had been removed and taken away by his killer. When word got around town that the killer had resurfaced, he was referred to among local children as Charlie Chop-off, due to the genital mutilation. The name garnered press attention and soon became synonymous with the rooftop killer.

Investigators believed the killer was dark-skinned, as a white man luring a black boy from East Harlem would have stood out. They began to focus on the fact he lured two of the victims to a rooftop. Though it was obviously more secluded, it would have been easier to take the boys to a basement or cellar.

They ran with the possibility that the killer wanted to claim his victims in full view of the city, and a rooftop was a perfect vantage point for it. For most investigators who worked on the case, it simply was a way to hide in the shadows.

People were more likely to report a man taking a boy into a basement that they were seeing them walk through an apartment building to the roof. After the press attention of the third attack, police hoped the killer would stop. They were wrong.

Five months later, on 7th March 1973, almost one year to the day of the Owens murder, another boy was murdered. Ten-year-old Puerto Rican Luis Ortiz went missing after an evening trip to a grocery shop in East Harlem.

The shopkeeper remembered seeing the boy but that he was short of change for the bread and milk his mother had sent him out for. The shopkeeper said it would be okay to pay the rest of the money the next day. But between the grocery store and his home, Ortiz disappeared.

The following day, he was found in the basement of an apartment block on the road back to his home. He had been stabbed 38 times in the neck, chest, and back, and his penis had been chopped off and taken away by the killer.

With three confirmed murders under the belt, and one brutal attack, the police finally confirmed there was a violent serial killer roaming the streets of New York. One who had a penchant for chopping off the penises of dark-skinned boys.

Based on the serial killer hypothesis, a large investigation got underway. Police checked all ships that had docked in New York at the time of the murders. When the ships turned up nothing solid, they began to believe the killer may have already served time in prison or a psychiatric hospital.

When police told the press they had linked the murders of the boys to one killer, a crowd of 500 angry residents descended on the police station. They demanded more protection for their children and the police obliged by placing officers at local schools and areas were children played, in the hope the killer would turn up.

But the locals told police that their children were scared to go to school and even carried knives for protection. Teachers began telling stories of their pupils playacting at lunchtime, pretending to be a killer chopping off their friend's genitals.

One young girl even wrote a story about a man killing boys and cutting off their fingers. The fear of Charlie Chop-off had spread so far that some psychologists linked it to mass hysteria. Children were told that if they were bad, Charlie Chop-off would get them, and it quickly became an urban legend.

Like many horror stories told to children, they sometimes manifest as real characters. And it was the children themselves who came up with and shared the moniker of Charlie Chop-off. Two weeks after Ortiz's murder, a mother from the Bronx called the police and told them the killer was most likely a man named Erno Soto, as he had been in and out of psychiatric institutions.

Police questioned her and Erno's family but he had been missing since November 1972 and didn't fit the description given by the surviving victim. However, the woman would later be proven right as the killer was indeed Erno Soto. As he was not caught, he was allowed to kill again.

Another five months past with no more attacks, and to the anger of the residents, no arrests. But on 17th August 1973, the body of eight-year-old Stephen Cropper was found on the rooftop of an East Side tenement building.

He had been raped and slashed with a razor, causing him to bleed to death but his genitals were still intact. Police were unsure if it was the same killer due to the lack of stab wounds or penis removal, but everything else fitted the profile.

The murder had taken place on a rooftop, the boy was dark-skinned, and he had been sexually assaulted. It was too coincidental for it not to be the same killer. The killer had also carved an X into the boys chest, which some would later suggest marked the tenth victim, but it was never proven.

Over the coming weeks, a number of suspects were arrested including a suspected paedophile and a Puerto Rican immigrant. But their known whereabouts during the murders and timelines didn't fit, so they were released, much to the public's anger.

Then, on 15th May 1974, 35-year-old Erno Soto was witnessed abducting a nine-year-old Puerto Rican boy. Nearby members of the public accosted Erno until the police arrived. Due to Erno's wild mental state at the time, he was immediately sectioned to a police psychiatric ward.

When interviewed by police, he confessed to the murder of Stephen Cropper but had no recollection of the others. They discovered Erno had been in a psychiatric unit at the time of the murder. But as they dug deeper, the truth emerged.

Erno's hatred of dark-skinned boys emerged from the fact his wife had an affair with a black man resulting in a black baby boy. His wife gave him an ultimatum. If Erno stayed with her then he would simply have to accept the child.

As time went on, he began to hate his wife and the boy, and it manifested to the point that he wanted to kill black boys. He mutilated or removed their genitals as he didn't want them to reproduce. It was a hatred that had come to a boil over a period of many years, and it drastically affected his mental health.

His first stint in a psychiatric hospital was in 1969 at the Dunlop-Manhattan Psychiatric Center where he stayed for a year. He was described by a psychiatrist as a walking time bomb, who was prone to outbursts of extreme violence.

During 1972 and 1973, he spent various amounts of time in the same hospital, sometimes as a resident and other times as an outpatient. Despite some of the murders taking place during times when Erno was on the ward, the hospital admitted he would often leave of his own accord.

It meant that during all the murders, Erno was likely not in the hospital at the time they took place. Combined with the confession of Cropper's murder, it appeared the police had finally caught the then infamous Charlie Chop-off.

At a non-jury trial in 1976, Erno was found not guilty of murder by reason of insanity. He was transferred immediately to a maximum security psychiatric institution. The murders stopped after Erno was caught, and Manhattan breathed again.

Due to the acquittal, the murders of the four boys and the attack on the fifth boy officially remain open. Though, police are still certain Erno was the killer, as are many who look at the case today.

Charlie Chop-off disappeared from the public eye but is sometimes spoken about as an urban legend. Only the authorities know what happened to Erno, as he disappeared into the system, never to be seen again. Until whispers of Charlie Chop-off bring him back into the public domain.

The Murder of Colette Aram

A confident killer murdered a 16-year-old girl and escaped justice for 25 years until advancements in DNA technology captured him, in the first case to be profiled on Crimewatch.

On the last afternoon of her young life, 16-year-old trainee hairdresser Colette Aram spent the time preparing and baking cakes at her family home in Keyworth, Nottinghamshire, a large village six miles from the centre of Nottingham.

At 8pm on 30th October 1983, Colette left home to visit her boyfriend's house. He normally picked her up from her house but his car had been taken off the road as it required work. The 1.5mile walk normally took about 25 minutes, but by 10pm, when Colette hadn't arrived, the alarm was raised.

Phone calls were made between her boyfriend and family before they realised something bad must have happened. Fearing Colette had become involved in an accident, her family and friends began searching for her along the route but the cold bite of the October night proved a hindrance.

Police put out a missing person's report and suspected she may have visited a friend's house but all her friend's told them they had not seen her. Though her family thought an accident may have happened, they were not prepared for the truth.

At 9am on Halloween morning, Colette's naked body was found in a field a mile away from where she had been abducted. She had been raped and strangled to death, with her body posed in a sexually provocative manner.

When the missing persons case turned into a murder investigation, police increased their manpower and began seeking information from locals. Colette had last been seen ten minutes after leaving her home when she stopped and talked to a group of friends.

Ten minutes after, a resident in a nearby house remembered hearing a woman scream but was unsure if it was kids messing around or a genuine cry for help. The resident remembered hearing a car drive off immediately after.

Crime scene investigators collected as much evidence from the scene of the crime as they could, which would help them in the future when DNA technology had advanced. At the time, police had little to go on, with only minimal forensic evidence, no direct eye-witnesses to the abduction, or a suspect.

The case went cold quickly much to the public's anger and put Keyworth on the map for all the wrong reasons. Nine months later, in June 1984, the BBC released the first episode of a crime reconstruction and appeal programme called Crimewatch.

Colette's murder was notable for being the very first case to be featured on the show. The format of Crimewatch was to reconstruct as much information of a crime as possible, in the way that was agreed upon by police.

As a result of the programme, Nottinghamshire Police received 400 calls, some of which claimed to have seen a car leaving the village at high speed. The programme allowed police to eliminate over 1,500 suspects.

But aside from wiping the suspect list, and various other tips, most of the calls led nowhere and the killer had seemingly got away with it. The case was run a second time on Crimewatch's 20th

Anniversary show in 2004, but again, the case was already as cold as ice.

The killer was 25-year-old Paul Stewart Hutchinson, a youth worker who had a liking for young girls. On the day of the murder, he had spent hours in a shed near a riding school close to the village, waiting for girls to start walking home alone.

His heinous plan was to lure one of them into the shed and rape them. He had already approached two girls that morning who told their families a man had acted strangely around them. It was reported to police only after the murder became public knowledge, but by that point, Hutchinson was long gone.

When he failed to select a victim, he stole a Ford Fiesta and drove around the country lanes, hoping to find a girl walking out in the darkness alone. At around 8.20pm, he pulled up next to Colette and proceeded to speak to her before jumping out of the car and abducting her at knifepoint.

He bundled her into the back seat of the car and smashed a bottle over her head before driving to a secluded location and raping her. He then hit her with the bottle multiple times before strangling her to death.

After killing her, he moved the body to the middle of a nearby field and posed her body, for reasons that never became known. Many suspect he was attempting to trick police into thinking he was a serial killer and that if he posed the body a certain way, the police would be looking for someone else.

Hutchinson didn't stop there, and out of a morbid curiosity, had returned to the village to watch the police investigation amidst the supposed anonymity of the crowds on 31st October, while wearing a Halloween mask.

A few days later, he sent a letter to police that read; *'No one knows what I look like. That is why you have not got me. You will never get me.'* For many years, the letter proved to be true but under the old adage of 'never say never', justice would finally catch up with him, 25 years later.

To cover his tracks, Hutchinson told his family he had cancer, and shaved his head, blaming it on chemotherapy, which was a lie. In the years that followed, Hutchinson believed he had escaped justice, and was able to work with children with learning disabilities.

In 2008, and because of advances in DNA technology, police were able to use the carefully protected forensic evidence from the crime scene and put together a DNA profile of the killer. At the same time they appealed for members of the public to report anyone they thought might have been involved in the murder.

The appeal didn't work but in June 2008 the DNA database returned a hit – which immediately didn't make sense. A man called Jean-Paul was arrested on a traffic offense and a DNA swab was taken at the police station.

His DNA was a near-identical match to the murder suspect profile drawn up by forensics. The police had their man, after 25 years, they could finally seek justice for Colette's murder, except, Jean-Paul had been born five years after the murder took place which instantly ruled him out.

The DNA match provided police with the clues they needed to solve the case and learned that Jean-Paul was the son of Paul Stewart Hutchinson, which is why the DNA profiles were so similar. Police arrested the then 50-year-old Hutchinson at his home the same day.

But Hutchinson, ever the confident murderer, had already developed a story to get the police off his scent. He claimed that the true suspect was his own brother who had passed away six months earlier and had been cremated.

Fortunately, for police, the hospital where his brother was staying before his death had taken blood samples, which didn't match the DNA profile of the killer. Hutchinson still pleaded not guilty but changed his plea to guilty on the advice of his lawyer.

In January 2010, 26 years after Colette's murder, Hutchinson was convicted and sentenced to a minimum of 25 years, one for each of the years he believed he had gotten away with murder. A week after his murder, Crimewatch returned to the case.

With the new evidence and killer behind bars, Crimewatch put out a new show featuring the case. In it, they were able to retrospectively look at the inconsistencies with their original programming and point out errors that had been made.

They also discovered errors in the media's reporting of the murder, including that Hutchinson was a psychology graduate, which he wasn't. Some of the inconsistencies in their programme may have resulted in Hutchinson getting away with the murder at the time.

Crimewatch was a vital investigatory and appeal component of major crimes in the UK, but due to declining viewership, the BBC cancelled the programme in 2017. Various spin-offs continue to run on broadcast television.

Ten months after his conviction, and suffering from depression, Hutchinson took an overdose of prescription medication and was found dead in his cell on 10th October 2010.

For Colette's family it was a heavy blow as it appeared Hutchinson had chosen not to live out his punishment. They were also hoping he would one day confess to the murder and explain why he had taken away their loved one, as he had never given a reason.

Colette's case shows that despite the passage of time, justice will inevitably find a way, and those who have committed historical crimes will forever be looking over their shoulders.

Killer Author

A detective reads a self-published fiction novel and discovers similarities to a real murder three years earlier, along with clues in the book that only the real killer would have known.

Wroclaw in southwestern Poland is the largest city in the historical region of Silesia with a population of over 1.25million. Sitting on the banks of the River Oder, the area is popular for non-commercial fishing, with many fishermen dangling their rods into the current, hoping for a decent catch.

Murder is considered a rare crime for a city of its size, but on 10th December 2000, a group of fishermen discovered a body on the banks of the river near a weir. It was immediately clear from the condition of the body that murder had washed up on the riverside of Wroclaw.

Police identified the corpse as that of a local businessman named Dariusz Janiszewski who had disappeared four weeks earlier, reported missing by his wife. He was the owner of a small advertising agency in the heart of the city, his business was going from strength to strength, and his disappearance was out of character.

When pathologists examined the body they found he had suffered a particularly brutal death. His hands had been tied behind his back with the same length of rope that weaved around his neck in a noose, in such a way that any movement with his hands would have forced his neck back.

Janiszewski was found with broken bones and a bruised face, the result of a lengthy and sustained beating. The examiners also found signs his limbs had been forcibly stretched to inflict severe pain. On top of all that, he had been starved, tortured, and stabbed to death before being stripped and dumped in the river.

Not a usual day for police in Wroclaw but a case that would result in the most unusual of conclusions. It was a murder that would become synonymous with a work of fiction in which the author would weave clues only known to the killer himself.

It turned out that Janiszewski had no known enemies, was well-liked within the professional community, and had run a successful business. The motives behind his murder were difficult for police to ascertain, and for the first two years, they came up with nothing.

After a six month investigation, the case went cold and was left unsolved, something that angered Janiszewski's family and friends. But with no evidence to go on, no witnesses, and no way of moving the investigation forward, the police had to temporarily close the case.

In early 2003, a little over two years later, a Polish crime show reconstructed the murder and aired it on national TV. It brought the case into the spotlight but resulted in multiple dead ends.

Reconstructions of crimes on shows such as Crimewatch, though generally lined with good-intentions, tend to result in false witness accounts, exaggerated theories, and a raft of phone calls to the investigating police station that can in some cases cause more problems than solutions.

In the case of the Janiszewski murder, police began receiving emails from all over the world. Various messages came in from South Korea, Indonesia, and Japan, among others, describing the case as the perfect crime and that it would never be solved.

Things quietened again until the Autumn of 2003, when Chief Inspector Jacek Wroblewski took over the cold case file from local police. It was known as the coldest of cold cases, and one the local police were happy to rid themselves of. Jacek was known as Jack Sparrow by his colleagues due to the translation of his Polish name to English, and his propensity to dress-down in the office.

He immediately concluded the murder was a result of someone having a deep grievance against Janiszewski, rather than being a random act of murder or a robbery. As he delved deeper into the files, he began to link things the original investigation had missed.

Janiszewski's mother had given a statement, that on the day of her son's disappearance, a man had called his advertising business demanding to speak to him. Janiszewski's mother said that she could help him with his requests but the mystery man insisted he specifically wanted Janiszewski to deal with him.

She gave the man her son's mobile number and thought nothing of it until her son went missing. Janiszewski showed up at the office later that morning and said he was meeting the man on the phone in the afternoon. He left the office at 4pm, left his car in the parking lot – and turned up dead four weeks later. It was the only lead Wroblewski had to go on.

Realising that Janiszewski's mobile phone had never been found, he began a search of the serial number of the device and discovered it had been sold on an internet auction site only four days after the body had washed up.

The seller was listed as 'ChrisB', who was in fact a self-published author and photographer named Krystian Bala. Initially, Wroblewski thought it too convenient that a murderer would have listed his victim's phone online on a public site, and so Bala was discounted as a suspect – until Wroblewski looked deeper.

Bala had moved abroad to South-East Asia, penning himself as a travel writer and blogger on the side, which meant he wasn't easy to reach. Wroblewski hunted down a copy of Bala's recently published book named 'Amok'.

Wroblewski found the book to be sadistic, pornographic, and creepy, with a murder of a woman and dark passages of prose. When he compared the real life case to the description of murder in the book, there were shocking similarities.

'I tightened the noose around her neck.'

This was one of the lines from the book that made Wroblewski sit up and take notice. The main character narrating the story was called Chris, the same name Bala used to sell Janiszewski's phone on the auction site. Already the similarities were mounting.

Bala, it seemed, was a law unto himself and used various philosophies and writings to create his own version of how life should be lived. He boasted about drunken visits to brothels and submissions to temptations of the flesh, both heterosexual and homosexual.

He told friends that he was capable of anything and that he would not live long but live furiously. By 2000, a few months before Janiszewski disappeared, Bala had filed for bankruptcy and ended his marriage.

His wife, Stasia, claimed they had been separated for quite some time, and Bala had taken to travelling as a means of escape, often visiting the United States and Asia, where he was known to have taught English. While he travelled he worked on his book; Amok.

'God, if you only existed, you'd see how sperm looks on blood.'

'I'm a good liar because I believe in the lies myself.'

'I pulled the knife and rope from underneath the bed, as if I were about to begin a children's fairy tale.'

'With my other hand, I stabbed the knife below her left breast. Everything was covered in blood."

The book was self-published in 2003, half a year after he had finished writing it, and three years after Janiszewski's murder.

Wroblewski began to focus on various passages and descriptions in the book as points of interest. Though the main character killed a woman and not a man, the description of the murder was similar, including the noose and the knife.

The character of Chris also sold the knife on an internet auction site a few days after the killing, which mirrored the selling of Janiszewski's phone – a snippet of information that had never been released to the public. Chris also alluded to killing a man who bothered him.

Wroblewski gathered together a group of colleagues to interpret the book page by page. They kept what they were doing quiet and did not speak to Bala or his friends and family. Because Bala was out of the country, they didn't want to spook him before they were certain.

As they went through the book, they discovered similarities to Bala's life, including various early criminal records, relationships, and businesses he had run.

A criminal psychologist who was asked to draw a conclusion on the book, wrote of the main character; *'His way of functioning shows features of psychopathic behaviour. He is testing the limits to see if he can actually carry out his sadistic fantasies. He treats people with disrespect, considers them to be intellectually inferior to himself, uses manipulation to fulfil his own needs, and is determined to satiate his sexual desires in a hedonistic way.'*

The psychologist warned it was common for novelists to have overlaps with their real lives, and that basing an analysis of an author from their fictional character would be incorrect. More importantly, a work of fiction was not evidence at all.

Wroblewski used Amok as a road map to a crime and started to link real-world people and descriptions to the fictional world of the book. They found another clue when Bala's buyer account had watched the listing of a book called '*Accidental, Suicidal, or Criminal Hanging.*'

In the early Autumn of 2005, Bala returned home and was brought in for questioning by Wroblewski, who was certain that Bala was the killer they were looking for. Bala simply claimed the book was fiction and any similarities to the murder had only been added through his imagination, a coincidence at best.

When questioned on the listing of Janiszewski's phone, he claimed he had bought it in a pawn shop but wasn't sure where, as it had been five years earlier. With nothing solid to hold him on, the police let him go. Bala went straight to the press and claimed the Polish police had kidnapped and beat him while attempting to get a confession.

A short while after, Wroblewski discovered that Bala's passport proved he had been in South Korea, Indonesia, and Japan, when the emails were sent to the Crimewatch-style show in 2003, claiming the murder to be a perfect crime. The passport stamps, along with IP addresses on page views of the murder's appeal page, suggested it was Bala who had sent the emails.

But Wroblewski and the investigation needed a motive. Bala going public, though frustrating to the investigation, was also a godsend. Witnesses had started to come forward. A friend of Bala's wife, Stasia, was in a nightclub with her in the Summer of 2000 when she saw Stasia on the dancefloor, dancing with none other than Janiszewski.

Two weeks after the murder, Bala and Stasia were at a bar when a bartender began flirting with Stasia.

Bala become angry and threatened to kill the bartender, claiming he had recently killed a man for the exact same reason.

When Wroblewski finally got to interview Bala's former wife, who had refused up until that point to talk anyone, he discovered the motive. Even though they were separated at the time, Stasia claimed that shortly after the nightclub incident, Bala had drunkenly smashed down her door and beat her.

Bala had apparently hired a private detective to watch her and Janiszewski, and discovered they had been having an affair, though none of this has ever been proven. But for Wroblewski, it was motive.

In 2007, Bala was put on trial for the murder of Janiszewski but pleaded not guilty as he believed the evidence was circumstantial at best. Despite no witnesses to Janiszewski's kidnapping and ultimate murder, Bala was found guilty. After a retrial in December 2008, he was found guilty again and sentenced to 25 years in prison.

In prison, Bala is known to be working on a second novel, and with evidence found on his computer, police believe he is tying the book into a second as yet unidentified victim.

'There's never been a book quite like this.' – Bala.

Jack the Stripper

If Jack the Ripper has gripped imaginations for over 100 years, then the story of Jack the Stripper in 1960s London, is enough to send chills to the darkest parts of your soul.

In comparison to countries like the United States, the United Kingdom has very few serial killers, and even fewer unsolved cases of serial killers. One of the most famous of the unsolved serial murderers is the Jack the Ripper story which has gripped imaginations for over 100 years.

But between 1964 and 1965 in West London, six prostitutes were strangled to death and their nude bodies discarded in or near the River Thames. Despite intense scrutiny in documentaries, books, and new imaginations, the murders have never been solved.

Here we look at the true story behind one of London's – and the UK's – most notorious, yet little spoken about unsolved serial killer cases. The press came to call him Jack the Stripper, and the murders were collectively known as the Hammersmith Nude Murders.

Though there were two prior murders that were later linked to Jack the Stripper, we'll look at the spate of six first.

Victim number one was 30-year old Hannah Tailford, found on the Thames foreshore in Upper Mall, Hammersmith on 2nd February 1964. The Northumberland-born woman was found nude with some of her teeth missing and her underwear stuffed into her mouth. She had been strangled and drowned.

Victim number two was 25-year-old Nottinghamshire-born Irene Lockwood, who was found dead in Duke's Meadow, Chiswick, on 8th April 1964. She had been strangled and drowned and was left nude on the foreshore of the Thames. Lockwood was pregnant at the time.

Victim number three was 22-year-old Scottish born Helen Barthelemy who was strangled to death and left in an alleyway in Brentford on 24th April 1964. A sex worker since the age of 16, she was found partially nude with torn clothing.

Victim number four was 30-year-old Mary Fleming from Scotland. Her nude body was found in Chiswick close to the Thames on 14th July 1964. She had been strangled to death. Nearby residents had heard a car reversing shortly before the body was found.

Victim number five was 21-year-old Frances Brown whose decomposing body was found in a car park in Kensington on 25th November 1964. She had been strangled to death and dumped partially nude. A friend and colleague of Brown claimed she had been missing since October after last being seen getting into a client's grey Ford Zephyr.

The sixth victim in the spate of six, was 27-year-old Bridget O'Hara, whose nude body was discovered on the Heron Trading Estate in Acton, on 16th February 1965. She had been drowned and her body displayed near a small electric substation. Bizarrely, it appeared her body had been kept warm before being dumped.

Though the six victims are considered to have been carried out by the same person, there were two prior murders that have since been linked over time. Both bearing remarkably similar traits to the six above.

The first of the additional victims was 21-year-old Elizabeth Figg, she was found in the early hours of the morning by two police officers on their regular route on 17th June 1959.

She was found partially nude on the north bank of the River Thames at Duke's Meadow, Chiswick. It was a familiar location to the officers, as prostitutes used the park as a place to take their clients. Irene Lockwood, the second of the spate victims, was also found in Duke's Meadow.

Elizabeth had been strangled to death. Her body had been found with her dress torn to the waist and ripped open to expose her breasts. Her underwear and shoes were missing and were never found. She was identified after a post-mortem picture distributed to the press was recognised by her mother.

She was also known to have carried a white handbag which was never found. It was suspected in the initial investigation that she had been murdered in a car and then her body disposed of on the shrubland near the Thames.

A local pub landlord, who lived on the other side of the river, claimed he had seen carlights in the area after midnight and may have heard the scream of a woman.

On 29th September 1963, 22-year-old Welsh prostitute Gwynneth Rees was found dead in Mortlake. She was found at the Barnes Borough Council household refuse disposal site, close to the Thames.

She was completely nude aside from a single black stocking hanging off her right foot. Gwynneth suffered an additional dishonour in death when workmen accidentally decapitated her with a shovel when flattening the rubbish.

By the death of Helen Barthelemy, the third of the six, police were beginning to suspect they had a serial murderer on their hands. Helen's death gave them their first clue, which were flecks of paint used in car manufacturing.

The same type of miniscule flakes were found at the scene of Bridget O'Hara's murder. Police believed the flakes to have come from the killer's workplace and spent a lot of the early days attempting to trace it to local businesses.

By the Spring of 1965, two months after the last murder, the police had interviewed over 7,000 suspects but still had no idea who the perpetrator was. They had managed to match the paint flecks to a concealed transformer, located near to where O'Hara was found.

A paint spraying shop was located on the same industrial estate which meant the flakes could have been lifted up in the middle of the night and placed at some of the crime scenes to throw the investigation off the scent. The paint clues and the constant interviewing had led them nowhere – at least, not yet.

Due to mounting public pressure and intense media scrutiny, the police decided to play a dangerous game with the killer.

Chief Superintendent John Du Rose of Scotland Yard was the detective put in charge of the Hammersmith Nude Murders investigations. He and his team had exhausted all avenues and decided to put pressure on the killer through a series of bluffs.

In the Spring, Du Rose held a press conference where and his team announced the police had narrowed down the suspect list to just 20 men. He said that by using an ongoing process of elimination, each suspect was being purged from the investigation until they got down to one.

But Du Rose was calling the killer's bluff. Despite interviewing over 7,000 suspects, they were no closer to catching the killer at all. The investigation decided that at the very least they could put pressure on the killer not to kill again and even force a surrender.

A few days later, Du Rose held another press conference and claimed they had narrowed the suspects down to ten. Another few days passed and another press conference took place where conveniently the suspect list had decreased to just three.

Though the crimes remain unsolved, the Hammersmith Nude Murders stopped and the unidentified killer seemingly vanished into thin air.

At the time of the murders, and in the decades that followed, many suspects have been named, with some being more plausible than others.

Shortly after the press conferences, a 57-year-old caretaker named Kenneth Archibald walked into Notting Hill Police Station and confessed to killing Irene Lockwood. He was eventually taken to trial but pleaded not guilty, claiming he had lied about the confession. He was later acquitted but the false confession meant police may have let the real killer get away.

In three books about the killings, *Jack of Jumps* by David Seabrook, *Found Naked and Dead* by Brian McConnell, and *Laid Bare: The Nude Murders and the Hunt for 'Jack the Stripper'* by Dick Kirby, the authors point towards a member of the Metropolitan Police as the suspect.

Seabrook claimed that many senior detectives in the Met believed a former police detective was responsible for the killings. The officer has never been named and many researchers believe the Met covered up the involvement of one of their own, hence why it has never been solved.

Later researchers suggested many of the victims were known to engage in the underground party and sex scene. It was suspected some of the victims had appeared in porn films and were known to have mild connections to something called the Profumo Affair.

The Profumo Affair became a major scandal when John Profumo, the British Secretary of State for War, was revealed to be having an extramarital affair with 19-year-old model Christine Keeler. The investigation into the affair unveiled tales of sex parties and underground porn, ultimately ending the Macmillan Conservative Government in 1963.

The theory was that some of the victims may have had information that could have further damaged the British Government. Thus they were killed off to make it look like a serial killer did it, to silence them and throw the investigation off the scent.

Du Rose maintained the killer was a Scottish security guard named Mungo Ireland, who worked on the Heron Trading Estate where the final victim O'Hara was found. He claimed the flecks of paint at some of the crime scenes were because Ireland worked near to where the paint spraying shop was.

When Ireland's name was mentioned as a possible suspect, he took his own life through carbon monoxide poisoning. A later investigation revealed that Ireland had alibis stating he was in Scotland at the time of all the murders.

The former British light-heavyweight boxing champion Freddie Mills was accused of being the killer in research for a book by gangster Jimmy Tippett, Jr. He claimed that many London gangsters knew Mills was the killer.

This was corroborated by a freelance journalist named Peter Neale who told police he had received word that *'Mills did it'*. Despite the suspicion, Mills was found shot dead in his car in the Summer of 1965. Though reported as a suicide, some believe he had been murdered to cover up the truth.

Back in 1921, Welshman Harold Jones had killed two girls from his hometown. On 21st June, he raped and killed 8-year-old Freda Burnell. 17 days later he killed his 11-year-old neighbour Florence Little. Jones was just 15-years-old at the time of both murders.

He was arrested and handed down a life sentence, but released 20 years later in 1941, at the age of 35. In 1947, Jones was known to be living in Fulham, London. Records show that he left Fulham in 1962, and his whereabouts between 1962 to 1965 – the time of the Nude Murders – remains unknown. Jones died in Hammersmith in 1971.

Due to poor police record-keeping at the time, he was never considered a suspect when the initial investigation began. A BBC documentary in 2019 called *Dark Son: The Hunt for a Serial Killer*, concluded there were many similarities between the murders Jones had committed as a boy and the Jack the Stripper murders.

The murder of a prostitute is especially difficult for police and other law enforcement. The very nature of the victim having had sex with multiple men and the interactions with hundreds, if not thousands of strangers, makes it even harder to investigate.

They are also less likely than most rape or assault victims to report the crimes to police for exactly the same reason.

There was a belief that law enforcement agencies wouldn't even worry too much about prostitutes being murdered and saw them as lower-class citizens. Another reason was that some officers throughout history had used prostitutes themselves and didn't want anything linking back to them.

Record-keeping and crime detection in the 1960s were far more difficult and disorganised than they are in today's digital world. Improvements in evidence collection and statistical data processes are at a far greater level nowadays.

Simply put, in the early to mid-20th Century, it was easier to get away with serial killing than in later decades, partly because victims were easier to find.

Jack the Ripper continues to dominate tours of London, and the Yorkshire Ripper continues to make headline news, even after his death. Why is it that the murder of eight women in West London, the clear work of a serial killer, doesn't reach the headlines as often?

Did the Met cover up the real name of the suspect to protect themselves? Were government officials involved in silencing prostitutes for fear of repercussions? Was Harold Jones unable to relinquish the dark desires of his youth and ultimately get away with eight more murders?

Many records of the case are still on file with the police, including evidence collected from the bodies. Even with advances in DNA technology, new investigators are struggling to connect the dots and to agree on a suspect.

Despite periodic checks by the Metropolitan Police, the case remains cold, and is subject to speculation at every turn. We may never know if the police bluff worked – or simply forced the killer so far underground that there was never any chance of him being caught.

The Horrors of Snowtown

In Snowtown, a master manipulator convinced others to help him commit serial murder and dispose of their victims' bodies in barrels of acid, leaving 12 dead, and a town forever tainted by infamy.

Before 1999, Snowtown in Adelaide, Australia, was known for its location on the main road and rail routes between Adelaide and Perth. With a population of a little under 500, the region relied on its crop economy and nearby salt mine.

That all changed when the town became the location where the remains of eight bodies were found in barrels of acid kept in a disused bank vault. Though only one of the murders took place there, Snowtown quickly found itself becoming a hub for true crime enthusiasts and dark tourism.

Between 1992 and 1999, John Bunting, Robert Wagner and James Vlassakis killed at least 12 people between them. A fourth member, Mark Haydon, was convicted on conspiracy to murder as he had helped dispose of the bodies.

Each of the victims had been dismembered and left to rot. Most of the victims were the killer's own family members or acquaintances that one of them knew. The discovery and resulting trial made Snowtown famous for all the wrong reasons.

The Snowtown Murders, more commonly known as the Bodies in the Barrels, are one of the most infamous cases in Australian history, a series of killings carried out by three serial killers, operating as part of a gang.

John Bunting, born in 1966 Queensland, claimed that each of the victims were either paedophiles, gay men, or simply considered inferior, traits that angered him. He made the others believe that murder was the right way to do things, to rid the world of true evil, as he saw it.

Before they killed their victims, they subjected each of them to horrific torture. All the victim's identities were stolen, and their bank accounts were emptied. Bunting was the ring-leader of the serial killing gang and instigated all of the murders.

When he was eight-years-old, he was violently beaten and raped by one of his friend's family members. The abuse he received was linked to him wishing to kill those who attacked children, and he made it his life's mission.

In Australia, the slang for a paedophile is rock spider. In one of the rooms of his home, Bunting created a rock spider wall of information, where he stuck the names and photos of people he suspected to be paedophiles or gay men.

He bundled gay men under the same rock spider banner, as he saw them as immoral and dirty, and linked to child abuse. He had managed to convince himself that gay men were as bad as child abusers, and that any men who showed weakness should be punished.

Bunting was known to be socially active and easy to talk to, this allowed him to bring people in close and manipulate others. This gave him a level of control over others who wanted to help him out or do things for him, but his darker side would shine through more often than not.

When he was in his early twenties, he worked at an abattoir and bragged to his friends and family about how he could skin and slice up any animal with ease. His love of butchery carried over into his everyday life.

He once killed a friend's dog simply because he wanted to see how the body functioned, claiming he was curious about the anatomy of animals and humans. He also told others that he skinned cats alive and enjoyed slaughtering animals whenever he found the opportunity.

In 1991, Bunting and his new wife moved to North Salisbury in South Australia, where his animal killings escalated into human murder. The first murder took place in 1992.

Bunting invited 20-year-old Clinton Trezise over for a drink at his place and accused him of being a paedophile. After a fiery argument, Bunting beat Trezise to death with a shovel, and buried the body in a shallow grave, it was a murder that paved the way for Bunting to claim more lives.

Clinton's body was discovered two years later in 1994 near the tiny town of Lower Light, but due to the decomposition, there was little evidence to suggest how he had died or who had killed him. It was later never proven that Clinton was a child abuser.

His was one of two bodies not found in the barrels or in Bunting's garden. The other was Thomas Trevilyan, who was found on the same day he had been killed in November 1997, again with little evidence pointing to a suspect.

It led many researchers to suggest that Bunting would use the paedophile or gay angle as an excuse to kill, and as a lure for the other men he roped into killing.

Bunting's neighbour, Robert Joe Wagner, was befriended by Bunting in 1991, and was encouraged to take part in the murders from 1995. At first, Robert thought he was helping as a vigilante but as time went on, Bunting's murders became less focused, and incredibly violent.

Wagner had just ended a relationship with Vanessa Lane, a transgender woman with a history of paedophilia. Formerly Barry Lane, they had started their relationship when Robert was only 14. The age gap was something that later enraged Bunting.

Bunting was married to Elizabeth Harvey, who had a son from a different marriage named James Vlassakis. He convinced James to help him kill those who deserved it, and James also went on to suggest victims. It was later discovered that Elizabeth assisted in at least one of the murders.

Mark Haydon lived near to the Bunting household, and he too was befriended by Bunting, and brought into his circle of killers and torturers. Haydon's cousin, Jodie Elliott, also helped out with claiming insurance and welfare benefits. With the gang growing in size, the murders escalated.

The next murder was in December 1995, when 26-year-old Ray Davies was tortured and murdered. A full victim list along with their statistics is available after the bibliography at the end of this book.

Many victims were subjected to horrific torture. This included knives, ropes, gloves, pliers, a shotgun, metal rods and an electric shock tool, which was used on the genitals of the men they killed.

On some of their victims, they crushed the toes with pliers, shoved lit sparklers into their genitals, burned their ears and nose with cigarettes, and beat them with clubs and metal rods. The killers ordered their victims to refer to them by many controlling names, including Master, God, or Lord.

Some of the victims were killed in their own homes, and the gang would rampage through their houses, smashing things up before killing them. They would also trash the homes of other people they believed to be gay.

Most victims however were lured to Bunting's home, where they were tortured before being dismembered. One of these was Vanessa Lane, Robert's ex-partner, who they decided deserved to be killed for having involved herself with Robert at such a young age.

It was Robert who instigated much of the torture on her. Lane's new partner, Thomas Trevilyan, who was part of the group for a short while, was also killed just weeks after Lane in 1997. One of Bunting's ex-girlfriend's was also killed, along with Elizabeth Haydon, Mark's wife. Many of the gang ended up killing members of their own family.

The group also tortured and killed James' friend, his half-brother, and the final victim, James' stepbrother, David Johnson. By this point, the group had rented a disused bank building in Snowtown. To hide the remains of their victims, they stored them in barrels full of acid, which they moved around to avoid detection.

James had lured the final victim to the bank building where the others were waiting. They tied him down and told him to read from a pre-written script, which included fake crimes and false confessions of things that Johnson had never done. They went to empty Johnson's bank account from an ATM and when they returned, he had died from his injuries.

This upset Robert, who claimed they hadn't made the most of their time torturing him. To appease him, everyone helped dismember Johnson's body and sliced off parts of his flesh, then they fried the body parts and sat down to feast on Johnson's remains.

Eight of the bodies were found in giant plastic barrels that were full of acid. Two of the bodies had been pushed into just one of the barrels. They stored the barrels in the old bank vault, and Bunting would return to them on regular occasions to see how well they were being dissolved in the acid.

Bunting said, '*they're rotting very nicely*,' when remarking on the first victim to be put in a barrel. He enjoyed watching the bodies dissolve and made notes on how long it took each body part to rot away.

Though David was the last victim, the group were ultimately caught as a result of the investigation into the disappearance of Mark's wife, Elizabeth Haydon. She had been killed because Bunting claimed she had made sexual advances towards him and he saw this as immoral and dirty – thus she needed to die.

She was killed without Mark knowing about it. When he was shown the body in the barrel, Mark reportedly huffed and smiled to himself. Enquiries into Elizabeth's disappearance ultimately led investigators to the old bank where they found the barrels.

Police suspected the group moved the barrels around to avoid detection, mostly because they knew they were being investigated. When police searched Bunting's home, they found two more bodies buried in his garden.

On 21st of May 1999, Bunting, Robert, James, and Mark were arrested on suspicion of murder. The subsequent trials were among the lengthiest and most expensive in Australian history.

Bunting showed no remorse for his crimes and spoke about the torture of the victims in such an open manner that three of the jury members walked out with their hands over their mouths. He also ignored the proceedings, instead reading a book, and refusing to listen to what was going on around him.

They were all sentenced in 2003. Bunting received 11 life sentences without the possibility of parole, for the murders of 11 people. The body of his ex-girlfriend, Suzanne Allen, who was killed in 1996, was found shortly after the barrels were discovered.

Due to her case being tried beforehand with suspects who were innocent, it was decided not to try her case again due to the agreed conclusion that Bunting had killed her, and that it wouldn't affect his overall sentence. Hence why Bunting was convicted of 11 murders and not 12.

Robert got life without the possibility of parole for his participation in nine murders. For his involvement in the crimes, Jamie was sentenced to life with a 26-year minimum term, after striking a plea deal to testify against Bunting and Robert.

Mark got 25 years in jail with a minimum term of 18 years. He struck a plea deal where he would not be charged with murder, but for helping the group of serial killers dispose of some of the bodies. Other people involved who helped in some way, struck plea deals to testify against Bunting.

It's not uncommon to read about serial killing couples or pairs, but rarer to find a case about a gang of serial killers. Bunting was at the heart of the mission to destroy gays, paedophiles, and weak men, and he was able to manipulate other men into killing as part of his mission.

Snowtown is now synonymous with the murders, and at one point, the community had voted to change the name to Rosetown, but for whatever reason, it didn't happen. However, the murders gained such infamy that tourist shops in the area began selling Snowtown murder souvenirs.

The rise of dark tourism and true crime enthusiasm meant that some shops in Snowtown never stopped selling bizarre souvenirs related to the murders. With the salt mine and crop industry giving diminishing returns, the dark tourism one unexpectedly took off, and solidified Snowtown's place in true crime infamy.

The Collector

There is perhaps no serial killer more inhuman than The Kansas City Butcher, who inflicted such terrible tortures on his victims that the term 'monster' has never been so appropriate.

This story is rather grim and contains descriptions of torture. It's included because Berdella remains one of the nastiest killers of the modern era and it remains bizarre due to the level with which he abused his victims and how he willingly carried out such tortures upon them.

On 23rd June 1987, Kansas, Missouri based serial killer Robert Andrew Berdella Jr. dragged a sedated 20-year-old Larry Wayne Pearson into his basement. He then violently tortured Pearson for the next six weeks before beheading him and dissecting his remains in August of that year.

Pearson was the last of six victims to fall foul to one of America's evilest killers, who would become known as either the Kansas City Butcher, Bob's Bazaar Killer (due to having a shop at a market), or The Collector (a film that influenced him to kill).

Berdella was the eldest son of a deeply religious family, with an Italian Roman Catholic father Robert Andrew Berdella Sr. and American mother, Mary Louise. Raised in Ohio, Berdella was sent on religious education courses and attended the local church for mass.

During his childhood he was afflicted with various impediments that saw him bullied in school and beaten by his father. When he was young, his father rarely allowed him to socialise outside of religious sermons and family chores.

As such, Berdella became a loner and was known to have been socially awkward. When he was five-years-old, he was diagnosed with near-sightedness and had to wear thick-rimmed glasses. Combined with a speech-impediment, he withdrew from society at an early age.

In doing so, Berdella didn't follow in his younger brother's footsteps and take up sport, instead becoming lethargic and gaining weight. Because of this lethargy, his father would often compare him to his younger brother, belittling him for not being like his other son.

Although Berdella's father abused his children he would pay particular attention to his eldest son. He emotionally and physically abused Berdella, sometimes beating him with a leather belt around his genitals and buttocks.

As he reached his teenage years, Berdella became confused about his sexuality, which he kept to himself, and despite finding a girlfriend, finally came out as gay in his late teens. On Christmas Day 1965, when Berdella was 16, his then 39-year-old father died of a heart attack while at home.

Berdella turned to religion in the hope that faith would somehow see him through what he described as a difficult time, regardless of his father's abuse towards him. When he didn't find what he needed, he began reading up on other religions and soon started to lose faith in what he had been taught as a youngster.

At around the same time, he had turned his withdrawal into a mask of exaggerated confidence. He became difficult to be around due to his new rudeness and attitude towards others, believing himself to be superior to those around him.

Then he saw a 1965 British-American film called *The Collector*. In the case of Berdella, it was one of the first known instances of a movie directly impacting the thought processes of someone who had the potential to kill and would go on to kill.

The plot of the film is about a man who abducts women and holds them captive in his basement to add to his collection. It is a direct correlation to the exact process used by Berdella in his future murders, except that he chose men instead of women.

Berdella directly cited the film as an influence of how he could kill. The Collector was also said to have influenced the American serial killing duo Leonard Lake and Charles Ng., who together in the mid-1980s killed at least 11 people but were suspected of 25.

The pair built a bunker and a self-built torture-chamber in a secluded area of forest which became home to a number of elaborate torture machines to 'play' with their victims. But even their crimes paled in comparison to Berdella's

Two years later in 1967, Berdella moved to Kansas and went to the Kansas City Art Institute where he was known to have become a promising student, but things quickly took a turn for the worst. After falling in with the drug crowd, he started to abuse drugs and alcohol, and even began dealing to other students.

Some serial killers torture small animals in their childhood years, because of an ability to overpower small animals where they can't overpower human abusers or carers. Berdella started late and used art as an excuse for torturing animals.

As part of his art, he used sedatives on a dog to witness the effects, then tortured and cooked a live duck in front of other students – for art. After making notes on his experiments, he left the institute after widespread condemnation but no authority was contacted about it.

He was arrested a few months later in possession of Marijuana and LSD. It is unclear whether the LSD was the Orange Sunshine Acid which is the type that Charles Manson and other known criminals went on to use.

Orange Sunshine was created and sold by a group going by the name of The Brotherhood of Eternal Love, who operated at a Los Angeles beach resort. One of its dealers, Ronald Stark, had known connections to the CIA.

The same batch of Orange Sunshine was available four months later at a free concert held at Altamont Speedway. Four people died at what should have been a peaceful festival. One of them was stabbed to death by a group who had taken multiple tabs of Orange Sunshine.

Berdella stayed in Kansas and moved into the now infamous 4315 Charlotte Street, in the Hyde Park area of Kansas City. He enjoyed using male prostitutes and spent a lot of time in gay bars in the city, openly taking part in casual sexual encounters with other men.

He would spend time with drug addicts or homeless people and gain their trust by plying them with drink and drugs before allowing them to live rent-free in his home in return for sexual favours, some of which were forced upon the most vulnerable in society.

Ever since his teens, Berdella realised the benefits of becoming pen-pals with foreigners. He wrote letters to people all over the world including Vietnam and Burma, two countries that were very much off-limits to the Western world at the time.

In return he would receive photos of ancient sites and small items from those countries, and so his collection began to grow. In disregarding mainstream religion he had developed a belief and understanding in alternative religions and occult magic.

This would lead him to open a rather unique store in 1982, a booth at the Westport Flea Market called

Bob's Bazaar Bizarre, which was an antique and curiosity shop. It sold primitive art, Asian artefacts and jewellery, some of which had come from his pen-pals in Asia but much of it by stealing items to sell at the booth.

To subsidise his earnings at the flea market, which were constantly up and down, he started taking lodgers at his home and became friends with the son of one of his fellow booth operators, Jerry Howell. When Jerry was 19, on July 5th 1984, he became Berdella's first victim.

Berdella promised to give him a lift to a dance contest but instead drugged him with heavy sedatives, took him home and tied him to his bed. Over the next 24 hours, Berdella raped, tortured and beat Jerry, then abused him with various household objects.

Jerry died after the drugs stopped his heart and he gagged on his own vomit due to the pain of the abuse. Berdella then dragged the body to the basement to try and resuscitate him but instead suspended the body from the feet.

As Jerry's body was hanging upside down, Berdella cut his throat and other arterial veins in order to drain the blood. He placed a large cooking pot underneath the hanging corpse to stop the blood spreading across the basement floor.

A day later, he returned to the basement and used a chainsaw and knives to dismember the body. He wrapped the larger body parts in newspapers and placed them in several trash bags around the city, which were collected shortly after and taken to the landfill.

We know all this in such great detail because Berdella had been keeping extremely elaborate notes and photographs of his victims and other assaults. His notes detailed each individual act of torture and abuse and outlined the intense physical and mental satisfaction that he gained from carrying out the murders in such a way.

If Jerry's murder was brutal then what followed was even more horrific. A year later in April 1985, 20-year-old Robert Sheldon begged to stay at Berdella's home after hearing how he helped people off the street.

Though Berdella initially agreed, he found Sheldon to be an inconvenience to his own lifestyle and drugged him before holding him prisoner in his bedroom. For three days, Sheldon was tortured in a variety of manners.

He was tied up with piano wire, had needles pushed underneath his fingernails, ears filled with waterproof sealant, eyes exposed to drain cleaner, and various parts of his body subject to burning and stabbing. Sheldon was suffocated to death after three days of torture and dissected in the bathroom.

In June 1985, Berdella lured Mark Wallace to his home where he was drugged under the pretence of providing him with a cure to his depression. He gagged Wallace then began torturing him in the bedroom. After needle torture and having an electrical device clamped to his nipples, Wallace died as his body went into shock – which frustrated and annoyed Berdella.

Three months later in September, Berdella met James Ferris who asked to stay at his home unaware of the torture chamber it had become. Like the others, Ferris suffered extreme abuse including being electrocuted until he couldn't sit up for more than a few seconds.

After extreme genital abuse and mutilation, Ferris's heart stopped and he died. He too was dissected in the bathroom. His fifth victim was Todd Stoop in June 1986, a man who provided sexual services in return for drugs – and Berdella was more than happy to oblige.

Once again, Berdella drugged and tortured him. Stoop was kept alive for two weeks and suffered horrendous pain from electrical shocks to the eyes, injections of drain cleaner into his vocal chords, and having his anal wall ruptured as Berdella forced his arm inside, causing him to die from shock.

Larry Wayne Pearson, the sixth and final murder victim, was one of Berdella's lodgers and Berdella hadn't planned on killing him. But after he bailed Pearson out of jail on 23rd June 1987, he made a crude remark about gay men, and Berdella saw red.

Berdella drugged him and dragged him into the basement – where the horror began. For the following six weeks until August 5th, when he finally killed him, Pearson was tortured and abused in the most horrific of fashions.

He would be injected with drain cleaner and had piano wire tightened around his wrists to cause nerve damage. Berdella broke one of Pearson's hands with an iron bar and electrocuted him with an electric transformer to all parts of his body.

He kept Pearson in various states of sedation and moved him around the house, including the second bedroom where he would rape and abuse him further. Towards the end, Pearson summoned the energy to bite Berdella's penis during a session of forced fellatio.

Berdella then beat him to death and later dismembered him in the basement. He stored Pearson's head in the freezer before burying it in the backyard. Although Pearson was his last murder, another victim escaped his clutches in March 1988, leading to his downfall.

22-year-old Christopher Bryson managed to escape from the house after three days of escalating abuse. When Berdella went to work, Bryson burned through his restraints and jumped from a second floor window, wearing nothing but a dog collar around his neck.

He broke his foot when he jumped but managed to cry out for help. Someone heard him and called the police, and Berdella was subsequently arrested on a search warrant after Bryson told them everything that had happened.

During the search of the property, investigators found 334 Polaroid images and 34 snapshot prints of his victims in various states of torture, before and after death. They found a human skull in the closet, a severed head in the garden, teeth in an envelope, and human spines in the hallway, though most of the larger body parts had been disposed of in landfills.

The basement was bloodstained and showed traces of flesh, hair, and brain matter. They found a chainsaw covered in blood with flesh parts in-between the teeth. But the main pieces of evidence used to convict Berdella were the detailed torture logs he kept on top of his cupboard.

In the summer of 1988, Berdella pleaded guilty to Pearson's murder and was sentenced to life imprisonment without the possibility of parole. He was also sentenced to an additional life term for the rape and assault of Bryson.

In September 1988, Berdella pleaded not guilty to the additional five murders. But his defence struck a plea deal that Berdella would plead guilty to one additional count of first degree murder, and four counts of second degree murder. The judge accepted the plea and sentenced Berdella to an additional five life sentences to run concurrently.

Investigators found a possible link to a total of 20 murders but only six could be verified using Berdella's notes and confessions. While in prison, he tried to convince interviewers and investigators that he had made mistakes and was not the demon he had been made out to be.

On 8th October 1992, while incarcerated at Missouri State Penitentiary, Berdella died of heart failure, much to the satisfaction of the family of the victims. Due to the widespread national attention the case had received, a local businessman purchased Berdella's home from the state and had it demolished as soon as he was in possession of the ownership papers.

Though we read many stories about the crimes of Ted Bundy, Jeffrey Dahmer, and Richard Ramirez among others, there is perhaps no serial killer more inhuman than the Kansas City Butcher, who committed the most atrocious acts against his fellow humans.

Playboy Bunny and the Schoolgirl

A Playboy Bunny and a schoolgirl were attacked and killed in two separate incidents in London six months apart, by the same killer who has never been identified.

Two murders in 1975, six months apart, were connected 30 years later by DNA evidence. London Playboy Bunny, Eve Stratford, was killed in Leyton on 18th March, and schoolgirl Lynne Weedon was killed six months later on 3rd September. Both murders remain unsolved and have haunted their respective families and cold case investigators to this day.

Eve was born in Dortmund, Germany, in 1953 to a German mother and English soldier, and she went on to win various beauty contests in the area in her childhood and early teen years. After travelling around the world with their jobs, the family finally settled on Aldershot in Hampshire in 1972, when Eve was 18.

In the same year, Eve hooked up with Tony Priest, who was the lead singer of English psychedelic rock band Onyx, who were active from 1965 to 1971. They quickly became close and Eve moved into a flat with him and two other band members in Leyton, North London.

In 1973, when she was 19, Eve became a waitress at the Playboy Club in Mayfair, which exists to this day. She had big ambitions of becoming a model and would aim to achieve that goal by using any means necessary. She quickly became a regular at the club and was known to be the favourite of the club owners, who paraded her around to attract customers.

Photos exist of Eve mingling with the likes of comedians Eric Morecambe and Sid James, and boxing legend John Conteh. Eve was so intent on becoming a model that she fought hard to feature in Playboy's American magazine. When she was turned down, she managed to be featured in the British rival to Playboy, an adult magazine called Mayfair.

Under the stage name of Eva Von Borke, she posed topless on the front cover as Miss March for the Spring Bonanza issue in 1975. She was pictured across nine pages with full frontal nudes, in an edition that sold almost half a million copies.

Due to appearing in Mayfair, the boss of the Playboy club suspended her for three months but it was suspected her killer had already selected Eve as a victim due to her appearance in the magazine. She would be killed just days after the magazine hit the shelves.

The boss of the Playboy club claimed that Eve was happy with the suspension as she believed the Mayfair spread was the stepping-stone to a greater modelling career. He was reported as saying that *'she wanted to do something with her life, and not wait on tables forever.'*

After posing for Mayfair, Eve took part in two more photoshoots, one for a South African pornographic magazine and another as a model for a crime novel, in which she was displayed semi-nude with a knife pressed against her throat, in a grim foreshadowing of what was to come.

On Tuesday 17th March 1975, just days after Mayfair hit the shelves of every newsagent in the country, Eve left her agent's office to walk home to her apartment. She arrived at around 4pm and was heard talking to an unidentified man by a neighbour.

The same neighbour heard a thud 30 minutes later as if something or someone had been thrown to the floor followed shortly after by footsteps coming down the stairs and out of the property. The neighbour never saw who it was.

Approximately 15 minutes later, Eve's boyfriend, Tony, and one of his bandmates, arrived home to a bloody crime scene. Eve had been tied up at her wrists and ankles and viciously raped. She had been stabbed in the neck 12 times, with the wounds being so severe they had almost decapitated her.

A bunch of flowers she had brought herself on the way home were found in the hallway of the flat. In less than 30 minutes, an unidentified man had raped and killed the ambitious model, leaving a crime scene that shocked London. Six months later, the same killer struck again, this time raping and killing a 16-year-old schoolgirl.

On Wednesday 3rd September, 16-year-old schoolgirl Lynne Weedon went on a night out with friends to celebrate their school exam results in Hounslow. They stayed in the local Elm Tree pub for most of the night until last orders were called.

Just after 11pm, Lynne started the ten minute walk home alone but someone had followed her from the pub. As she turned into an alleyway known as

The Short Hedges, she was hit in the back of the head and fell to the ground. The attacker lifted her up over a high fence and threw her into an electricity substation.

Lynne was dragged away from the fence, raped, and beaten with a heavy blunt instrument which was never recovered but thought to have been a lead pipe. The alleyway, close to the local school, was notorious for people hanging around after dark but no murder had ever taken place there until Lynne's.

The following morning, the caretaker of the school, whose house overlooked the substation, looked out his window and saw Lynne's body on the ground. Despite her horrific injuries, which included having a fractured skull, Lynne was alive when emergency services arrived at the scene.

Unfortunately, she never regained consciousness and died in hospital a week later on 10th September, which led to a murder enquiry being opened. Two witnesses claimed to have seen a white man running away from the scene at around the time of the murder but it was too dark to make an identification.

At around the time of Lynne's murder, Eve's murder was still being investigated. Police concluded that the Mayfair spread had tempted her killer because the attack was sexual in nature and due to the magazine being released a few days before her death.

The apartment had not been broken into and the neighbours heard no shouting or screaming, which suggested that Eve knew her attacker. In 1970s London, tracking someone's postal address would have been easy, privacy laws were very different back then.

In the Mayfair spread, Eve spoke of her bisexuality and how she liked being dominated sexually by men and how she enjoyed playing games with her lovers. She also said she lived alone with her cat, which wasn't true as she lived in the flat with her boyfriend and his bandmates.

The nude photos, the preference of being dominated, the statement of living alone, a known club where people could see her work, all led to Eve being selected as a victim. The flowers found in the hallway suggested that her killer had either followed her home or was waiting near to the entrance and accosted her by the front door.

It's possible that Eve knew her attacker as a customer at the Playboy club or maybe she was overpowered as soon as the front door opened. It seems more than likely that she was overpowered due to the flowers on the floor.

Other workers at the Playboy club were interviewed and one of them claimed she had received death threats by phone after she appeared in a similar adult magazine. Eve was also known to have received mysterious phone calls where the caller would simply breathe on the other end and not talk.

In October 1975, a landlord was cleaning out a flat in Liverpool after it had been vacated by two male tenants when he found something suspicious and called police. Newspaper reports of Eve's murder were nailed to the wall with darts and smeared with lipstick, and many pictures of her had been stabbed with the darts.

A year later, the investigation into Eve's murder ended, as police had exhausted all leads and had no evidence to go on. But the brutality of the crime would not go unnoticed and it would be another 30 years before her murder was linked with Lynne's.

Eve and Lynne's killer – or killers – would have been very strong. It would take a lot of strength to drag a grown woman up the stairs to her apartment and the same amount of strength to lift a 16-year-old girl over a high fence and throw her to the ground on the other side.

The killer slashed and stabbed Eve in the neck 12 times which almost caused a decapitation, which again would have needed considerable strength, it also would have been pre-planned, as Eve was killed after she was raped, most likely to stop the killer being identified.

Lynne was hit over the head with a heavy object, instead of being stabbed, and she would have been unconscious when she was raped. The killer then hit her again before leaving and assumed she would have died, but she wouldn't have been able to identify him as she was first hit from behind.

In 2004, cold case investigators reopened Lynne's case and looked at all the details but came up with nothing new. Then in 2007, due to advancements in DNA technology, investigators were shocked to discover that the same killer was responsible for both Lynne's and Eve's murders.

Which was unusual due to the manner in which they were killed and the different type of victims they were, one being an adult model and the other a local schoolgirl. The DNA didn't match anyone on the databases, and genealogy testing has proved fruitless.

A profile of the killer was drawn up and suggested he was a white male between the ages of 17 to 30 and may not have committed any crime beyond

1995, when DNA began to be collected from those alleged with committing crime.

Many psychiatrists and profilers have looked at both murders and claimed it would be unusual if the killer did not ever confess to anyone, and almost impossible to have kept a dark secret such as murder for so long. He was also thought to be someone local to Hounslow, due to his knowledge of the alleyway that Lynne took on that fateful night.

Both rapes and murders were premeditated and it seemed unlikely that the killer only claimed two victims. If he had killed again then he may have developed new methods to hide his victim's bodies or claimed a victim that has not yet been linked to him.

The possibilities relating to the two cases are endless. It's possible there was an error in the DNA testing, which has happened before, resulting in a contaminated test accidentally linking two bodies where there was no link. However, the DNA has been tested again for good measure and there is a match.

There could have been two killers, which would explain the strength needed to lift the victims, and maybe they both raped the victims with one taking extra precautions to not leave any evidence, but it seems unlikely as multiple rape/murders are rarely committed in pairs.

Despite the DNA evidence, some researchers and authors have pointed to the killer as Peter Sutcliffe but the DNA evidence does indeed rule him out. There is also the belief that Eve's murder was covered up as it may have been someone famous and well-known from the Playboy club but again it wouldn't explain why Lynne was murdered, unless to go all-in on the cover-up story.

There are a large number of cold cases in the UK but none quite as baffling as the murders of the Playboy Bunny and the schoolgirl. It appears that without new evidence, both cases will forever remain unsolved, and the killer will have got away with at least two murders.

Ossett Exorcist Murder

A loving husband, thought to be possessed by 40 demons, became the subject of an all-night exorcism, and less than two hours later; ripped his wife and dog to pieces with his bare hands.

Exorcism turned loving husband into killer! A true case of possession! The Ossett exorcist murder! So read the headlines in 1974 England, when 31-year-old Michael Taylor killed his wife by tearing her eyes and tongue out with his bare hands, following an exorcism by a local team of priests.

Born at the tail-end of the Second World War in 1944, Michael was raised in the English market town of Ossett in Wakefield, West Yorkshire. Though Ossett was very much a Christian town, the Taylor family were not overly religious and never found the time to attend the local churches.

Neighbours of the family described them as mild-mannered and full of kindness, despite their unwillingness for a religious life. Michael became a full-time butcher and married the love of his life, Christine, soon after.

By the early 1970s, the couple had five children and were living in a small rustic house in the town they'd both grown up in with their dog. Michael hurt his back in an accident that forced him to leave the butcher's job and struggled to find full-time employment afterwards.

He suffered bouts of depression which saw him becoming withdrawn from the community and he became less social with those around him. This caught the attention of one of his friends, Barbara Wardman, who believed the only cure for his depression was religion.

Barbara introduced him to a church group called the Gawber Christian Fellowship, despite Michael not attending church regularly. He attended the first group meeting with Christine, and both were so impressed with the group's outlook on life that they converted straight away.

When Michael's depression began to improve after a number of group meetings, his friends and members of the church believed it had improved purely on the basis of spiritual intervention and by the hand of God himself.

While at the church meetings, Michael became besotted with the 20-year-old lay preacher, Marie Robinson. A lay preacher is a preacher or religious servant who is not a formally ordained cleric and helps the church in the promotion and function of its beliefs.

Within a few months, their friendship had reportedly become 'carnal' – another way of saying they were intimately engaged. Marie's soft spoken leadership of the group was too much for Michael to ignore and he spent as much time with her as he could.

Soon enough, Marie held private meetings with Michael, where he would supposedly talk in tongues and made the sign of the cross with his hands for hours on end, believing it would quieten the dark and evil power of the moon; the opposite to the light and goodness of the sun.

Michael began joining in some of the sermons and helped cast out demons from other group members, even though neither Marie nor Michael were trained exorcists. They were simply using their positions to empower themselves.

A few weeks later, members of the group met at Michael's home, and Christine voiced her opinion that Michael was spending too much time with Marie. Michael then forced Marie upstairs where she rejected his advances before re-joining the group.

When Marie rejected him in his own home, Michael's attitude changed and he became argumentative with Christine at every opportunity. He withdrew back into depression, acted irrationally and developed a bad attitude towards the church group.

Then Michael attacked Marie in full view of the group. He rose from his seat, and stared at her with wild, bestial eyes, and a look of a man intent on killing. Marie began screaming out of fear at the sight of him but Michael grabbed her by the shoulders and neck and shouted at her in tongues.

Marie called upon the name of Jesus, and the other members of the group managed to restrain Michael, who had no memory of what had gone down. Concerned he was becoming possessed by a demon, the congregation called on a local priest and his wife to intervene.

Peter and Sally Vincent invited Michael to their home for an assessment where Michael threw their cat out of a window and broke some pottery in anger. After witnessing his anger and actions, the Vincent's put together a team of people to help in an exorcism at the church.

On 5th October 1974, as the midnight hour dawned, Michael was summoned to St. Thomas Church where he was restrained and underwent a seven-hour exorcism. Peter and his team burned Michael's crucifix, pushed wooden crosses into his mouth, doused him with holy water and screamed at him to dispel the demons.

At the court case following the murder, Peter confirmed they had exorcised a total of 40 demons who had taken residence within Michael. Coincidentally, the only demons they couldn't exorcise were those associated with murder, violence, and insanity.

The priests told Michael not to worry about the other three demons and that they would exorcise them at a later date, so he was sent home. Less than two hours later, a policeman on a routine patrol through the town stumbled on a gruesome sight.

Michael was ambling along the street completely naked and covered head to toe in blood, screaming about the demons within him and Satan himself. The officer managed to restrain Michael and took him to a hospital, before heading to Michael's home where more police were outside.

Their neighbours had heard violent noises and already called police. When the officer arrived, a senior detective stumbled out the house and vomited in the front garden, telling him not to go inside as Christine Taylor had been ripped at and left in a mess.

In a possessed rage, Michael had killed his wife by tearing at her face and chest with his bare hands. He ripped out her eyes and tongue, and according to the autopsy report, had almost ripped off her entire face from her skull.

He had then strangled the family dog to death before tearing its body to pieces, ripping its limbs off and covering himself in its blood, along with the walls and floor. When Michael was arrested in hospital, he claimed that *'the evil inside her had been destroyed.'*

In an unprecedented trial, Michael was acquitted on the grounds of insanity. A defence psychologist posited the theory that Michael's actions were a direct result of the intense psychological torment he had suffered at the exorcism, and laid blame on the priests involved.

The priests who were brought in to testify stated they had expelled all but three of the demons and it was one of the three demons that had possessed Michael and used his body to kill Christine.

Though the trial didn't prove that Michael was possessed, it did lead to him being acquitted.

Michael was sent to the infamous Broadmoor psychiatric hospital for two years before being transferred to a lower-security facility for another two. He was released just four years after brutally murdering his wife and dog.

If any of this sounds familiar, the case was mentioned in the 2021 film *The Conjuring: The Devil Made Me Do It*, which is based on the 1981 trial of American murderer Arne Cheyenne Johnson, who claimed he was possessed by a demon.

The case was investigated by demonologists Ed and Lorraine Warren, who believed that Arne was indeed possessed. Arne was ultimately convicted of manslaughter and spent five years in prison. Demonic possession was never proven.

The exorcism of Michael Taylor raised many public questions that were never answered including why the priests in charge of the exorcism had never been charged with psychological damage, or why Michael was released only four years later.

Whether he was possessed, psychologically tortured, mentally unstable, or a cold-blooded killer, depends on one's own beliefs of the existence of the otherworldly, and that which can inhabit a human body and mind.

In 2005, Michael was arrested again for touching a teenage girl, and was admitted to psychiatric care – with the same symptoms as he had showed in the hours before he ripped his wife apart. Leading some researchers to suspect that a demon remains within him still.

The Unsolved Murder of Ann Heron

On the hottest day of the century, a woman sunbathing in her bikini had her throat cut by an unidentified attacker, then left in a pool of blood for her husband to find.

The UK's not really known for consistency in its weather patterns and seasons, but 1990 was a little different. On 3rd August of that year, temperatures reached a scorching 37.1C (98.8F), making it one of the hottest days of the 20th Century.

The usual things happened; people got sunburnt, suffered heatstroke, or drank too much alcohol and passed out in the sun, to wake up stuck to the stones on the beaches around the country. But in Darlington, County Durham, murder clouded the skies.

44-year-old mother of three, Ann Heron, like many others on that fateful Friday, was taking advantage of the weather and sunbathing in her garden. Unlike many others, Ann was brutally murdered by an unidentified killer.

Born Ann Cockburn in 1946 in Glasgow, she moved to England in 1984 when she met the love of her life, Peter Heron, who also had three children. They got married in a lavish ceremony and moved into Aeolian House, a large country property in Middleton St George, near to Darlington.

Ann was a part-time care assistant at a nursing home, while Peter worked as the CEO of GE Stiller Transport, a haulage firm on the outskirts of the town. They lived a happy life, with a growing family, solid social standing, and were well-liked in the community.

There was nothing in their lives that suggested a motive for what happened next but someone, whether by opportunity or planning, decided to end her life in the most brutal of ways.

Peter left the home and went to his workplace at the haulage firm, he arrived as always before 9am, such was his dedication to good time-keeping. An hour later, Ann, who had the day off, met up with a friend, Sheila Eagle, and went into Darlington centre to shop for items for a party later that day.

Just before 1pm, and as he always did, Peter went home and had lunch with Ann, no doubt discussing how hot the day was becoming. There's nothing the British like doing more than moaning about the weather, and there's good reason for it — it's unpredictable, and rarely consistent.

An hour later at 2pm, Peter left home to go back to work, leaving Ann to relax for the afternoon. Half hour later, Sheila phoned Ann to discuss details of the party, the call didn't last long and Ann was free after to that to soak up the rays.

At around 3.30pm, a friend of Ann's passed by the house on a bus and saw her sunbathing in the large garden. There was seemingly nothing untoward and no sign of the danger to come. 45 minutes later, Ann was spotted driving her car by a lorry driver and his passenger.

They knew Ann through her daughter, Ann Marie, and when they saw her car, they beeped the horn and Ann waved back. They remembered seeing one man in the passenger seat and another in the back but had no idea who they were.

At 4.45pm, a passing motorist saw a blue car on the driveway of Ann's home, which didn't belong to her. A few minutes later but before 5pm, another witness saw a blue van with two men parked up at the end of the driveway to the house.

At 5pm, Ann was murdered by having her throat cut, and her bikini bottoms were removed. Five minutes later, a passing taxi driver saw a tanned man in thick trousers running away from the house, estimated to be in his thirties.

The driver also noticed a blue car speed down the driveway, screech into the road, and head towards Darlington town centre. At 6pm, peter returned home from work to find the front door open and made his way to the sunbed in the garden.

Beside the empty sunbed on a small table, the radio was still playing, and a cigarette was in the ashtray, along with a half-drunk glass of wine. Peter went back into the house and found Ann lying face down on the living room floor in a pool of blood.

Police arrived within minutes and kickstarted one of the biggest manhunts in County Durham's history. At first, due to the couple's mild wealth and luxury country house, robbery was put forward as the motive behind the attack, except the house hadn't been robbed.

Sexual assault was the next motive to look at but despite Ann's body missing her bikini bottoms, there were no signs of abuse. Two theories relate to the bikini bottoms, one was that due to the heat she was sunbathing partially nude or was wrapped in a towel, and the second was that her killer removed her bikini bottoms to make it look like she had been sexually assaulted when she hadn't been.

Ann had her throat cut with a very sharp blade that a coroner suspected may have been a razor, she had also been stabbed in the neck, either with the same blade or a different one. The attack had severed a major artery and Ann's blood soaked into the floor around her body, leading one officer to call it a bloodbath.

There were no signs of a struggle or forced entry, which meant that Ann most likely knew her killer, unless someone had approached her while she sunbathed in the garden, which meant the doors to the property would already have been open.

Unsurprisingly, the investigation looked to the then 55-year-old Peter as the main suspect. Detectives uncovered an affair between Peter and a younger barmaid at the Dinsdale Golf Club that he frequently visited, which would have given Peter motive to murder his wife.

It was also suspected at the same time that someone close to the barmaid may have found out about it and decided to punish Peter by killing Ann. However, in the days following the murder,

Peter's colleagues confirmed that he was at work at the time of the murder, thus giving him a solid alibi.

He also didn't look like the person running away from the scene and refused a solicitor on the basis that he hadn't done anything wrong. He remarried three years later in 1993 in a private ceremony, but not to the barmaid he was having an affair with.

Despite the alibis, lack of forensic evidence against him, and no real motive, Peter was rearrested in 2005 and charged with Ann's murder. Durham Police's infatuation with Peter being the killer may have let the real killer get away with murder.

Unsurprisingly, the case against Peter was dropped in the same year due to a lack of evidence, which meant Durham Police were clutching at straws. Peter's children and family claimed the case had been damaging to him and that Durham Police had failed to meet a good standard of policing which had compromised the quality of the investigation.

And not without just cause, for the police didn't look into the blue car until many years later, and other suspects were not considered at the time due to their fixation on Peter and trying to make the evidence fit him as the killer.

By the Spring of 1991, the case had gone cold, despite many press conferences in which Peter pleaded with the killer to come forward, and a Crimewatch UK reconstruction for TV. Then, in early 1993, a woman reported an unusual story to police.

She claimed that a man had walked into the card shop she was working at, and in conversation with her boss, boasted about killing Ann. The woman claimed that her boss had taken the man into the back room to discuss bulk purchases.

The boss came out of the stock room with a pale white face, as the man walked past him and out the front door. The boss relayed the story to her and said the man would never be caught as he was moving to Australia the next day. The man was never found.

In late 1994, The Northern Echo newspaper and Durham Police received multiple letters from a man claiming to be the killer. He wrote how much he enjoyed killing Ann and the rush he got from it. Though the source of the letters have never been traced, experts have debunked them as fiction.

Aside from the 2005 misstep that led to Peter's arrest, the last big update on the case came in 2020, when the then 85-year-old Peter hired a private investigator named Jen Jarvie. He concluded his investigation by saying that the killer may have been a violent criminal on the run from prison, a man named Michael Benson.

Benson was a convicted criminal with a history of robbery and assault, and one attack with a carving knife. During the summer of 1990, Benson was released from prison on licence but failed to report back and went on the run.

He also owned a blue car similar to the one seen in the driveway of the house. He was rearrested not long after and was never considered a suspect at the time, though he had been questioned about his whereabouts on that day. He died of natural causes in 2011.

Many oddities surround the case and the official timeline, with many questioning the reliability of the witnesses. The lorry driver who had seen Ann at 4.15pm, said he had beeped his horn and Ann waved back at him.

This meant, that according to other witnesses, Ann was sunbathing in her bikini at 3.30pm, driving around town fully clothed with two men 45 minutes later, and then back in a bikini an hour after that, near the time she was murdered.

It's possible the lorry driver didn't see Ann with two men and only thought he did. Driving a lorry on the hottest day of the year would have made it difficult to keep focus on everything. The driver's statement wasn't given until many weeks after the murder.

At least two witnesses put a blue car near to the house or in the driveway at around the time Ann was murdered, which suggests that the driver of the blue car could have been the killer, or at least aware of what had happened.

It doesn't explain the man running away from the house, but he could have been someone else in the car who disagreed with what happened or a runner wearing jogging bottoms, getting as sweaty as he could under the hot sun. But the big question remained – what was the motive?

There were no signs of robbery or sexual assault, despite Ann missing her bikini bottoms, and no signs of forced entry. Ann wasn't tortured or stabbed multiple times in a frenzy, she had her throat cut and the killer walked away, pointing to the fact he might have been a thrill killer or someone involved in a pre-meditated hit.

Some researchers point to the barmaid as instigating a hit on Ann, to get her out the picture so she could be with Peter but there has been no evidence to prove it. As a barmaid, it was possible she spoke to all kinds of people in passing and may have mentioned her distaste for Ann.

She had the best of both worlds; Peter's sexual attention but without the responsibility of his children. It seems a strange kind of hit for Ann to have her throat cut, which would have ultimately led to further forensic evidence than a more professional hitman would have left.

Two more theories remain. One that the man who confessed in the card shop was indeed the killer. Maybe he knew Ann and had made advances on her that were rejected. He drove to her house that day to convince her to be with him then killed her when she refused his advances.

The second was that the killing was opportunistic in nature which is why the killer has never been caught due to the randomness of it. While walking or driving past the house, the man – and it would have been a man – may have seen Ann sunbathing in the garden.

With the hot sun clouding his judgement, he perhaps took the violent decision to end her life. but again, this is mostly conjecture and theories. What we do know is that Ann Heron was killed for no apparent reason by an unidentified killer in a case that has never been solved. It remains County Durham's only unsolved murder of the 20th Century.

Stoned Butcher of Tompkins Park

A self-confessed marijuana guru dismembered his roommate, boiled the remains, and made soup from her brains – which he ate and shared with unsuspecting homeless people.

Tompkins Square Park is a public park in East Village, Manhattan. By the end of the 1990s, homelessness had reached an all-time high and there were said to be an estimated 80,000 homeless people around New York. According to 2021 statistics, that figure was still around 50,000.

The park was home to tent city, a zone where homeless people had set up camp. In 1989, a rumour began spreading that a local eccentric man named Daniel Paul Rakowitz had killed his girlfriend, consumed her then made soup with the remains which he fed to the homeless of tent city. The rumour turned out to be true.

Daniel was born in 1960 in Fort Leonard Wood, Missouri, to an Army criminal investigator and his wife. Due to his father's work, they moved around the United States and in the late 1970s settled in Rockport, Texas.

At some point in his young life, Daniel discovered marijuana and became a slave to its highs. In 1985, he moved to New York City where he embedded himself in the drug culture. A few months after arriving, he became homeless and began sleeping in tent city.

To get by, he starting selling pot but eventually found employment as a part-time cook, one of his passions. As his mind began to fracture, he founded his own religion he called the *Church of 966* – then brought a chicken and kept it with him everywhere he went.

Eventually, he was earning enough to afford a flat share with a young couple, Sylvia and Shawn, in East Village, for which he covered half the rent. He'd first met the couple when selling them pot on the edges of tent city. As he began to settle in the apartment, he began cooking for the homeless.

Most mornings, he would head to a local food shop and stand outside begging for food or money. People would buy him meats and vegetables and some days he would return to the flat with 10kg of food. Then he would cook it all up, separate it into tubs and take it to the homeless in tent city.

But when he wasn't spreading kindness and generosity, he was selling pot and spreading the word of his new religion under the influence of drugs. He attempted to convince his roommates he was the lord of the lords and that by 1992, his followers would take over the world.

Four years after that in 1996, he said he would become the president of a new regime. He was noted as saying, '*if they think Hitler was something, they haven't seen anything yet.*' However, Daniel had no followers as it was a delusion of the mind caused by excessive marijuana use and a newfound fascination with LSD.

He believed by feeding the homeless population, he held sway over them and that they had become his followers. On 20th July 1989, Sylvia and Shawn split up and they went their separate ways, leaving Daniel in the apartment alone seeking a new roommate.

Finding a roommate wasn't easy, as Daniel was more than eccentric and a little difficult to live with. He carried his chicken on his shoulder wherever he went and smoked pot all times of the day. To find his roommate, he began hanging out at Billy's Topless strip club.

The club was located in the Chelsea neighbourhood of New York City and was active from 1970 to 2001. It had become an informal landmark but many patrons viewed it as seedy due to the club owner's belief that real women should strip and not the barbie-doll type women who danced elsewhere.

26-year-old Monika Beerle was one of those strippers. She had come to America from Switzerland to study in teaching and choreography. Known to her friends as having a daring personality, she still had a level head and was seen as being smart.

She was already looking for a place to live when she met Daniel outside the club. After only a few hours of knowing him, she agreed to move in and pay half the rent. Daniel spent the next few days spring-cleaning the apartment believing that Monika was moving in with him as a companion and not a roommate.

When he told his friends in tent city, they warned him Monika would put her own name on the lease and kick him out. But he denied it, claiming he had fallen in love with her, talking about her all the time.

Monika shut down any sign of a romantic relationship with Daniel and began bringing men home to the apartment. One of them was a black man who Daniel hated. He began ranting and raving at Monika but she wasn't having any of it and told him he had two weeks to leave the apartment.

By that point, Monika had paid off rent arrears which Daniel owed, technically buying him out of the lease. He pleaded with her that he had nowhere to go but Monika was not stepping down. She wanted him out and that was the end of it – or it should have been.

A week before the murder, he told a friend that Monika was stupid to have messed with him and now he was going to kill her. Of course, none of the people he ranted to took him seriously but in his mind, it was the only logical way out of the situation.

A day before the murder, he contacted Sylvia and told her he was going to kill Monika and needed help moving the body. Sylvia ignored him, but the following night, Daniel made good on his word. When Sylvia visited the apartment two days later, she stumbled upon a horrific sight.

She opened the door to the apartment and couldn't see anyone inside but noticed something cooking on the stove. She wandered over to it and saw Monika's head in a pot, blackened from where it had been stewing.

Then, upon entering the bathroom, she saw the result of a brutal murder. There were body parts all over the place, including a ribcage with the flesh sliced off. The bath was full of blood and there were lumps of flesh all over the room. She quickly made her exit, not knowing where Daniel was.

She ran to a phone box and called Daniel's beeper to ask if he had done it. He confirmed he killed Monika but wanted to go back to the room with Sylvia and smoke a joint. Amazingly, Sylvia didn't go to the police and met Daniel at Tompkins Park where she listened to his entire confession.

Daniel explained what had happened. He had gone to a hardware store and purchased almost $100 of tools to kill Monika and dispose of the body. On the night of 19th August 1989, he walked up behind her and wrapped an extension cord around her neck, strangling her to death.

To make sure she was dead, he stomped on her head and stabbed her 30 times. He dragged the corpse to the bathtub and cut off her head before using her chest as a carving board. After slicing up pieces of her flesh, he admitted to eating parts of her brain raw.

He used a solid steel pole to break the bones then boiled the remains, some of which he flushed down the toilet. But he kept her brains in a different pot which he stewed and made into a soup with herbs and spices.

The following day, Sylvia returned to the apartment with Shawn, not knowing what to expect and not knowing what to do – though the obvious route to take was to report it. They entered the apartment to find Daniel smoking a joint next to Monika's skull.

The skin and flesh had been boiled off to make more soup. Daniel told them he would spit on the skull and curse Monika's ghost. He claimed she would always be with him and always have a home, and that she looked more beautiful than ever.

They noticed human flesh in the frying pan and body parts in the freezer. Daniel told them he had eaten parts of her body and really enjoyed it, especially the brain soup. So much so that he was going to make more soup and feed the homeless at the park.

Still, Sylvia and Shawn didn't go to the police, and for the next five days, Daniel would tell anyone and everyone what he had done. He made the soup as promised and delivered it to homeless people, who were unknowingly eating food containing human remains.

To some of his friends in tent city, he admitted the soup contained the brains and other parts of Monika's body but he was dismissed as an eccentric stoner. An entire month passed until Shawn decided enough was enough and went to the police.

On 18th September, police went to the apartment to search for evidence but Daniel was missing and had cleaned out the apartment. Graffiti on the front door read, '*welcome to Charlie Gein's spahn ranch east.*' Written below it was, '*is it soup yet?*'

Charlie Gein was a name Daniel had used to honour two of his idols, Charles Manson and Ed Gein. Spahn ranch was the commune of the Manson family. Daniel had moved in with another lady friend outside of Manhattan.

Which made the killing of Monika all that more pointless, as the sole motive was to avoid getting kicked out of the apartment. Police couldn't find anything in the apartment but arrested Daniel a day later. They found a duffel bag with Monika's bones and her skull.

When word got around Daniel had killed and eaten another human being, the demons from the past resurfaced. Some of his old schoolfriends told reporters he had killed a number of cats and at least three dogs. He had also starved one of his dogs before selling it for pot money.

Another claimed that if Daniel had any kind of personality or charisma then he could have formed his own cult and easily converted people. Instead, his cult became a cult of one and he went all in on his own beliefs, alienating others with his love of Hitler.

Daniel claimed there was a friend with him on the night of the murder, a friend he'd met at an unidentified Satanic church in the city. He couldn't name the church nor the friend, leading some psychiatrists to believe he had made up the friend to egg himself on and carry out the murder.

At the trial, Daniel claimed to have no knowledge of what happened from the point of strangling Monika to finding her body dismembered. On 22nd February 1991, the then 31-year-old Daniel was found not guilty of murder by reason of insanity.

He was admitted to the maximum-security Kirby Forensic Psychiatric Center. Sylvia and Shawn made a plea deal for a confession and were never charged with a crime. 13 years later, in 2004, a jury deemed Daniel no longer a danger to the public but that he was still mentally ill.

He was ordered to remain at Kirby Forensic indefinitely. He became known as either the Butcher of Tompkins Park, the Butcher of East Village, or the Tompkins Park Cannibal. It's bad enough to eat another human but to feed human soup to unsuspecting homeless people truly is something else.

Lesbian Vampire Killer

A lesbian lover of all things occult claimed to survive off the blood of animals before convincing her friends she was a vampire who needed to kill to satisfy her craving for the red stuff.

Multiple personality disorders have been given the horror entertainment treatment so many times it has become synonymous with having literal different personalities. Though there are similarities, it is an often misunderstood disorder.

Today, the condition is known as dissociative identity disorder (DID) and is defined by the presence of one or more alternate personalities, known as alters. It is characterised by identity fragmentation and not an army of different people living in the same body.

Which is why when an Australian murderer was diagnosed as having four to six different personalities, it was met with much scepticism. But for some researchers, it was proof that multiple personalities living in the same body was possible.

The murderer's name was Tracey Avril Wigginton, who on 20th October 1989, stabbed to death 47-year-old council worker Edward Baldock. She then partially severed his head and drank blood directly from his exposed neck.

The murder itself was as horrific as it was vampiric in nature, spurred on by her belief that she needed human blood to survive, to get stronger. A psychiatrist later conclude Wigginton had at least four personalities. On the night of the murder, it was a personality named April who came to the fore, named after her violent adoptive mother.

Wigginton was born in 1965 in Rockhampton, north Australia. At the age of three she was adopted by her grandparents following her parents' divorce. Her mother did not have the means or mental capability to look after her anymore.

Her grandparents were known to be abusive towards her and it was claimed she was sexually, physically, and emotionally abused. In her early teens, she began to gain weight and came out as a bisexual.

When she was 15, after her grandfather died, she attacked a man who had come to visit her grandmother. She fractured his nose and slashed his fingers with a kitchen knife, before violently pushing his hearing aid into his ear canal.

Her grandmother died in 1981 when she was 16 and she moved back in with her mother, only to find her mother did not accept her sexual preferences. When she received a $300,000 pay-out from her grandparents will, she moved in with a friend, and for a while, everything was going smoothly.

She was known as a loving human, gifted with the creativity of art, and attended the local church having become a devout Catholic. She met a young man and became pregnant by him but weeks into the pregnancy, she miscarried.

It led her down a dark path and she refused to attend mass at the church, in time blaming god for her lot in life. She came out as gay before venturing into the world of the occult. Before long, she had a craving for blood.

During her late teens and early twenties, Wigginton began to go deep into the occult, believing she was a vampire. To placate her vampiric desires, she visited the local butcher who supplied her with pigs and cows blood.

She allegedly warmed it up in a microwave and drank it from a cup. Other times, she lured local pets to her home before killing them and drinking their warm blood. She was also alleged to have killed a wild animal with a hunting knife and scooped the blood from the wound into her mouth.

Only months before the murder, she got into a relationship with Lisa Ptaschinski, a local woman one year her senior. To placate her new partner's desire for blood, Lisa would cut her arms and neck so Wigginton could slurp the blood from her open wound.

Two more friends, a lesbian couple named Kim Jervis and Tracy Waugh, were brought into her world of the occult and vampirism. Due to her large size, Wigginton was a domineering presence who convinced her girlfriend and the couple she had supernatural powers.

All three believed Wigginton was a vampire who could even make herself disappear. In the weeks before the murder, the four of them had a midnight picnic at a nearby cemetery, which resulted in them removing a headstone and taking it back to Wigginton's home.

The headstone took pride of place in the living room and gave Wigginton the impetus she needed to convince her friends further. She made them watch a notorious video nasty that showed real people being executed and told them she had been thinking of killing someone for their blood.

The night before the murder, Wigginton dyed her hair jet black and told her friends she needed to feed on a victim's blood, or she wouldn't be able to maintain her sanity, as much as it was.

They went out to a lesbian nightclub in Brisbane's Fortitude Valley called L'Amours. There, before the club was overrun with partygoers, Wigginton convinced them they needed to claim a victim for her to feed on. Together, they came up with a plan.

At 11.30pm, they left L'Amours and set off in Wigginton's car, to cruise the streets, looking for a man around the time the pubs kicked people out. At midnight, they spotted 47-year-old Edward Baldock staggering out from the Caledonia Club and followed him.

When he was alone, Wigginton pulled up beside him and lured him into the car with the offer of a good time. The drunk father of four went for the forbidden fruit and gave into temptation, falling into the back seat, ready for some fun.

Wigginton drove four miles away to Orleigh Park, an isolated area on the river in the West End, a place she knew would be deserted at that time of night. She parked up and took Edward with her into the darkness of the park, leaving the other three in the car.

Wigginton removed her top and told Edward to get himself ready as she went to relieve herself. But she went back to the car, grabbed the knife she had been sharpening for days, and told Lisa to come with her to watch.

Edward had stripped off and folded all his clothes into a neat pile when Wigginton walked up to him from the darkness and plunged the long knife into his neck. She then stabbed him another 27 times in the back and neck.

As his body fell to the ground, she ordered Lisa to go back to the car, as she got to work partially severing Edward's head. As he lay dying, she leaned in and drank the blood from the large open wound, savouring every drop she could.

After, she sat down next to the body and smoked a cigarette, later claiming to have '*felt nothing.*' Upon return to the car, Lisa and the other two could smell the blood on her breath. At 5am the next morning, a jogger stumbled upon Edward's body which had been left in the open.

Though Wigginton thought they had planned the perfect murder, they hadn't. Next to the body, police found a pair of shoes containing Wigginton's bank card, with her name on full display. She only realised she had left it the next morning.

She drove back to Orleigh Park to discover police had swarmed the area. She said to one of the friend's, '*oh my god, it's real.*' It was one of the instances in which she was thought to have had a personality disorder, as they are often categorised by amnesia and a sense of feeling detached.

The police arrested Wigginton and the other three less than two hours later, and within hours, they had confessed the truth of what had gone down. It was then that psychiatrists decided to assess Wigginton further – and some scary revelations came to light.

Wigginton agreed to be hypnotised. When she went under, she responded to questions using different voices and mannerisms. The main personality was Big Tracey, who was thought to be the dominant personality and an amalgamation of all of them.

Another was Bobby, a violent 16-year-old who hated the world. Little Tracey was a scared child but April was the one that terrified assessors. April was named after her abusive grandmother and would speak in a lower voice, claiming she needed blood to survive.

However, one assessor believed Wigginton was making the whole thing up and suggested she hadn't been hypnotised at all. She showed no remorse for the murder. The only thing she was sorry about was that she had been caught.

After being cleared fit for the courts, she and the other three went on trial for murder, with Wigginton the only one pleading guilty. She blamed the murder on her desire for blood and that it released a repressed rage from a childhood filled with abuse.

She said, *'it's scary to have that much power. It's playing god with life and death. Nobody should have that sort of power but we all do.'* Lisa and the other lesbian couple had become so convinced in Wigginton's powers they truly believed she was a vampire.

In 1991, Wigginton was sentenced to life in prison for murder. Lisa was also sentenced to life after a lengthy trial deemed her culpable in the murder. Kim Jervis got 18 years for manslaughter, later reduced to 12, and Tracey Waugh was acquitted for her part in the crime.

They all claimed the sole reason for the murder was to enable Wigginton to feed from another human. In 2006, Wigginton attacked a fellow inmate and prison guard during a row but was not brought to trial for it.

In 2008, 17 years later, Lisa was released under a resettlement program with a new identity. In 2012, after 21 years in prison, and much to the anger of the Australian public, the lesbian vampire killer, Tracey Wigginton was released on parole.

The release brought widespread criticism of the courts. A detective involved in the original case, said the murder was the most brutal and disturbing he had ever worked on. Edward's family were understandably completely against her release.

Despite the anger surrounding the release, Wigginton kept herself to herself afterwards. Until seven years later, in 2019, when she roared back into the news. After accessing a Facebook account under the name of one of her 'personalities', she posted the following two images.

After, she shared more photos of vampires, skeletons and real human remains. Despite calls for a return to prison, the parole board decided she had not violated her release conditions but confirmed she would remain under supervision for the rest of her life.

Which was of little relief to Edward's family and the lives of those she managed to control and ruin.

The lesbian vampire killer roams Australia today as a free woman, whose actions after her release prove there is no remorse, and that April may be simmering beneath the surface.

True Crime Killers Volume 4

As a thank you for adding this book to your collection, we would like to offer you a FREE eBook for simply signing up to our mailing list. Along with a free book, you'll get weekly updates from the world of true crime brought to you by truecrimelists.com, and early book release notifications so you can be the first to get them at an introductory price, exclusively for subscribers.

Visit WWW.TRUECRIMELISTS.COM and click on FREE BOOK from the menu.

www.ingramcontent.com/pod-product-compliance
Lightning Source LLC
LaVergne TN
LVHW051116080426
835510LV00018B/2071